AF531596

DYNAMICS OF RURAL LABOUR

About the Author

Babu P. Remesh is Reader at the School of Interdisciplinary and Transdisciplinary Studies, Indira Gandhi National Open University (IGNOU), New Delhi. He holds a Ph.D. (Economics) from Centre for Development Studies/Jawaharlal Nehru University. Prior to his joining IGNOU, Dr. Babu was Fellow and Coordinator, Integrated Labour History Research Programme and Archives of Indian Labour at the V.V. Giri National Labour Institute, NOIDA. He has many years of research experience in the fields of labour and development studies. He has to his credit several research papers published in reputed journals and books. He is author of *Shifting Trajectories: Work Organisation, Labour Relations and Mobilisation in Contemporary India* (2008). He writes a regular column on labour history, 'Labour in Those Years' in *Labour File*.

Dynamics of Rural Labour

A Study of Small Holding Rubber Tappers in Kerala

Babu P. Remesh

CONCEPT PUBLISHING COMPANY PVT. LTD.
NEW DELHI-110 059

The publication was financially supported by the ICSSR. The responsibility for the facts stated, opinions expressed or conclusions reached is entirely that of the author and the ICSSR accepts no responsibility of them.

The work was evaluated by Prof. S.T. Sawant (Advisor, The Ambedkar Institute for Labour Studies, Mumbai), on behalf of ICSSR.

ISBN-13: 978-81-8069-660-2 **ISBN-10: 81-8069-660-X**

First Published 2010

Published and Printed by

Concept Publishing Company Pvt. Ltd.
Regd. Office:
A/15-16, Commercial Block, Mohan Garden
New Delhi-110059 (India)
Phones : 25351460, 25351794, *Fax* : 091-11-25357109
Email : publishing@conceptpub.com,
Website: www.conceptpub.com

Editorial Office:
H-13, Bali Nagar, New Delhi-110 015, India.

Cataloging in Publication Data-- *Courtesy:* D.K. Agencies (P) Ltd. <docinfo@dkagencies.com>

Remesh, Babu P.
Dynamics of rural labour : a study of small holding rubber tappers in Kerala / Babu P. Remesh.
p. cm.
Revision of the author's thesis (Ph. D.)--Jawaharlal Nehru University.
Study conducted at Kanjirappally, Nedumangad and Perumbavoor taluks of Kottayam, Thiruvananthapuram and Ernakulam districts respectively of Kerala, India.
Includes bibliographical references (p.).
Includes index.
ISBN 13: 9788180696602 ISBN 10: 818069660X

1. Rubber tappers--India--Kerala. 2. Rubber plantation workers--Supply and demand--India--Kerala. 3. Industrial relations--India--Kerala. 4. Rural development--India--Kerala. I. Title.

DDC 338.476782095483 22

To my Parents.......

Acknowledgements

This book is a revised version of my Ph.D. Dissertation submitted to the Jawaharlal Nehru University. It is with a deep sense of gratitude, I recollect all those who have directly or indirectly contributed to the completion of my dissertation and the subsequent preparation of this book.

The research for this work was carried out at the Centre for Development Studies (CDS), Thiruvananthapuram under the supervision of Dr. K. Narayanan Nair and Dr. G. Omkarnath. I am indebted to both of them for their continuous support and encouragement at every stage of this research. I gratefully acknowledge the support, academic inputs and encouragement from several friends and faculty members at CDS.

I am grateful to Indian Council of Social Science Research and University Grants Commission for the Doctoral Research Fellowships awarded to me at the Centre for Development Studies.

My association with V.V.Giri National Labour Institue, as faculty, provided me rich exposure to labour issues. I consider this as a special fortune that sharpened my analytical skills and understanding on labour. Dr. Prabhu Mohapatra and Prof. Navin Chandra had been kind enough to spare considerable time in sharpening my research questions.

My sincere thanks to the external supervisors of my dissertation, Professors D. Narasimha Reddy and K. Nagaraj, who had given very encouraging comments on my work, besides highly recommending me to pursue the publication of this book.

My sincere thanks to the Indian Council of Social Science Research (ICSSR) for the award of publication grant, which enabled the publication of my research in its present form. I am deeply indebted to the ICSSR Consultant, Prof. S.T. Sawant, Advisor, The Ambedkar Institute for Labour Studies, Mumbai who evaluated the thesis for ICSSR. Thanks are also due to Dr. Prem Prakash Pandey of ICSSR for all the support. I also thank the Concept Publishing Company Pvt. Ltd., New Delhi, Mr. Ashok Kumar Mittal and his team for printing and publishing this book.

My thanks to Neetha and Appunni is obvious and needs no elaboration. 'We three' have been together during the crucial part of this journey and I am sure, all of us equally shared its sweet and sour moments. It is a pleasure that we are blessed with Kannunni, by the time of publication of this book. My families at Ponnani and Changanassery were extremely supportive in various stages of the dissertation. Especially, the inspiration and support from my parents, P.P. Achuthan Nair and P. Gouri Teacher, provided me the required strength and momentum towards continuing and completing my studies. I dedicate this book to their endless affection and support.

Babu P. Remesh

Contents

List of Tables

List of Figures

1

Introduction

Economic development of Kerala is largely linked to the transformation in its labour front and it is often understood to be driven by the moblilisation of working class. While in rest of India, both rural and urban wage-earning classes are mostly disorganised and largely excluded politically and economically, higher levels of mobilisation and socio-economic integration of the labouring poor has been a distinct feature of the state (Franke and Chasin, 1997; Isaac and Tharakan, 1995; Heller, 1999). This departure of Kerala from the national pattern primarily owe to the specific patterns of class formation and the institutional linkages that emerged from repeated cycles of class-based contestation and state intervention (Heller, 1999). The achievement of the state in terms of impressive progress in human development, despite the absence of concomitant levels of economic growth exemplifies a situation in which empowerment of the working masses have led to improved living conditions of the general population. This unique phenomenon, widely known as *'Kerala Model'* has been central to the development discourse of the state during the past three decades.

Background of the Study

The development experience of Kerala has attracted international attention, ever since the publication of the UN/CDS study in 1975, which highlighted the unique features of the widely proclaimed *'Kerala Model'*[1]. The study while elaborating the positive achievements of the state in human development, despite its lower GNP per capita *vis-à-vis* the rest of India and poor performance in industrialization, drew the conclusion that Kerala "has certainly some lessons for similar societies seeking social and economic advance" (UN/ CDS, 1975).

The widespread academic attention attracted by the *'Kerala Model' inter alia* resulted in a continuous documentation of the state's achievements in human development, since mid 1970s (Lindburg, 2001). Alongside, the paradoxical existence of higher levels of social development with unimpressive growth of GDP and per capita income was the central issue of concern in developmental thinking.

The commendable performance of Kerala in terms of human development could be attributed to a host of factors, which even date back to the social reforms and educational movements in the nineteenth century. However, among the myriad factors, the radical strategy of redistribution followed by the democratic governments in the state during the post-independence era is viewed as the single most important[2]. The successive governments in the state enacted and implemented several legislations[3] and welfare programmes for the benefit of the working class. Since the late 1960s, with the active participation of the state, several contributory welfare funds were initiated and managed in Kerala. These welfare funds, which cover a wide spectrum of labouring poor including agricultural workers, toddy workers, cashew workers, head-load workers, coir workers, handloom workers, construction workers and so on bring in almost all the rural and 'informal' sector workers under its coverage[4]. Nevertheless, to see the Kerala Model as an outgrowth of only of 'wise policies' of the state is to miss its most significant feature: the organisation, mobilisation, and active participation of millions of state's ordinary people in struggles to bring about these policies[5].

The mobilisation levels of the working class in Kerala were fairly high even at the time of formation of the state in 1956. By this time, the working class emerged as a recognisable electoral pressure group. As Heller (1995) notes: *"ever since its formation, 'class' was the centre of politics in Kerala"*. Due to the visible lenience of governments towards the demands of the labouring poor, the working class attained a dictating position in the formulation of public policy[6]. Considering the electoral strength of the workforce, every election manifestos of the political parties included more and more appeasing packages to workers, which eventually led to the shaping of the '*Kerala Model*'[7].

The major focus of the working class-oriented agenda of the governments was on expansion of social infrastructure, social security schemes and interventions to redistribute rural wealth. These intercessions included, among other things, introduction of land reforms[8], expansion of health and education programmes and strengthening of public distribution of food and essential commodities. By the 1980s, both in agrarian and industrial occupations, the status of workers in Kerala became impressive with higher wages; better working conditions and diverse social security programmes. In this backdrop, it is reasonable to believe that the higher human development in the state, which gained wider currency with the term, '*Kerala Model*', is the consolidation of redistributive gains by the working class in the post-independence period.

Crisis of 'Kerala Model'

Of late, there is a growing consensus among the scholars that Kerala at the moment is traversing through a phase of crisis, though various scholars give different explanations for this. While some commentators relate the crisis to Kerala's excessive dependence on a global capitalist system, structural adjustment programmes, a new liberal economic order, and growing culture of consumerism, there are also extremist assertions that the crisis is inevitable and built into the '*Kerala Model*', as its priority has been attached to social development and redistribution, leaving economic growth only as a secondary goal[9].

A widely accepted explanation of the crisis approaches it from the angle of growth performance of the state's economy and view slow growth in economic sphere as a serious and continuing problem to the overall development (Kannan, 1998). It was highlighted that Kerala's economy has grown at a much slower rate than the national average for most years since the late 1970s. Between 1988 and 1994, Kerala rebounded with an annual growth rate of 6.4 per cent compared to 5 per cent for all India (Heller, 1998) before slipping again in 1996-97 with a rate of 7.5 per cent as against 14.2 per cent for the national economy (Franke and Chasin, 2000). The weak economic basis of Kerala economy was given thrust in these explanations, referring to the stagnation in agricultural production until the late 1980s and the sluggish industrial growth since the mid 1970s till mid 1990s (Nandamohan, 1994; Subrahmanian, 1994; Isaac and Tharakan, 1995; Parayil, 2000). The underlying concern of the above approach was the issue of sustaining the scale of social development, given the bleak economic performance of the state.

Another skeptical note raised on the sustainability of the model finds it root on the acute and perennial fiscal crisis, which characterises the Kerala economy in the recent decades. It is cautioned that the continuing fiscal crisis in the state is bound to undermine many of the redistribution programmes, which include the pension schemes to agricultural labour, expenditure on education and health, and the public distribution system for food (George, 1993; Parayil, 2000).

Yet another explanation views the crisis, through a critical examination of the validity of the social development indicators, being conventionally employed in development economics, such as low infant mortality, high life expectancy, favourable sex-ratio, low birth and death rates, high literacy and so on. It is argued that if by social development we mean content of the society, perhaps the above indicators have little to do with the social development. For instance, there are several other indicators that reflect the discontent of the society such as high rates of suicides, divorce and mental disorders. In fact, Kerala has the highest suicide rate in India—three times the national average and 50 per cent more than the second highest state (Halliburton, 1998). Further, there are arguments to the effect that the achievements of the state in terms of maximum number of hospitals and hospital-goers could also connote the higher morbidity rate and prevalence of severe health problems in the state.

Irrespective of their approach towards the issue, all the above explanations question the potential of the state to sustain its achievements in human development, given the sluggish performance of productive sectors of the economy. This in turn attracted the attention of researchers to probe into the root causes of the crisis and one of the central concerns in this effort was to understand the linkages between development and political economy of labour in the state.

Situating Labour in the Development Crisis

As discussed earlier, the development trajectory of Kerala is highly intertwined with the dynamics of labour market in the state and most of the current development dilemmas in the state are increasingly understood to have strong linkages to the phases of labour mobilisation. Of late, it is widely observed that the influential positioning of the trade unions in the state had severely affected the growth of investment and thus employment in Kerala. By the mid 1980s, Kerala obtained the label of a 'problem state'[10], characterised by higher wages and increased 'labour militancy', which resulted in a situation of investors shying away and flight of capital from the state to neighbouring 'investor friendly' states such as Tamil Nadu and Karnataka (Albin, 1990; Kannan, 1998). Further, it has been noted that the state experienced a long run loss of employment due to halting of technological change in labour-intensive activities by the organised workers, for realising the short-term goal of employment protection. This resistance, along with the strong forms of wage rigidities backed by social stigmas attached to the undercutting of wages (Krishnan, 1991), is often viewed as an important aspect that deterred the growth of investment in Kerala since the 1970s. The excessive dependence of the state on remittances from abroad also questions the sustainability of social development in the state. It is observed that any decline in the flow of remittances from non-resident Keralites would adversely shake the state's economy with multiplier effect. Of late, there are also arguments which understand the sluggish growth of the commodity production sectors as the outcome of the state's failure to tackle the situation, by way of attracting investment from outside the state and converting the considerable loanable funds available through the remittances from abroad.

The reported mismatch between labour supply and labour demand, a phenomenon that gained wider recognition since the mid 1980s is another puzzle in the state's development discourse. It has been widely acknowledged that while certain sectors reported acute labour shortages, the unemployment levels have remained at higher levels, especially in the case of educated youths[11]. The increased tendency of the youth to shy away from manually demanding work as well as their resistance towards accepting employment at lower wages could also be seen as an imprint of the *'Kerala Model'*. On the one hand, higher educational status deterred the entry of youngsters into socially `demeaning' manual work. On the other hand, the redistributive policy followed by the successive governments in the state, enhanced the retention value of workers, leading to supply side rigidities in the labour market.

Yet another major aspect, that needs to be discussed while situating labour in Kerala's development crisis is the implications of large-scale international migration of Keralites, especially to the Middle East. Many of the achievements in the social sphere of the state (such as education and health) are closely linked to the regular flow of remittances from the Keralites working abroad. The contribution of remittances to the SDP rose steadily from a meagre 2 per cent in 1975-76 to 23 per cent in 1999-2000[12]. The internal labour market of the state was affected drastically due to the above stated high levels of migration. The high outflow of skilled and unskilled workers from Kerala, led to shortages and mismatches in the labour market, resulting in shooting up of both nominal and real wages. There was a steady growth of wages from the mid 1970s, which has gained further momentum during 1980s, following the construction boom facilitated by remittances from abroad. This migration has been an effective route for economic emancipation of poorer households, as it supported the sustenance as well asset creation (mainly in terms of housing and household amenities). Migration also helped in enhancing the reservation price of labour, and even deferred or deterred the entry of youngsters in the labour market, a phenomenon that further accentuated the labour shortages in select occupations, such as farm work and casual employment in rural areas.

On the whole, the foregoing discussion highlights the centrality of labour in Kerala's development process and in its present crisis. It also underscores the need for conceptualising the labour market dynamics of Kerala in the overall background of the state's political and socio-economic background.

Statement of the Study

A major puzzle that has been underlying the state's rural labour market is the paradox of simultaneous presence of high unemployment and higher wage rates. On the one hand, the state enjoys one of the highest wage rates in rural occupations, which is more than double the national average in all major rural occupations (Ministry of Labour, 2004); (Appendix Table 1.1). At the same time, the rural unemployment levels are strikingly high in the state. Further, when it is claimed that rural unemployment is rising in the state, acute labour shortages are reported in select sectors, especially in farm operations, in the sense that "*employers are willing and are actually seeking to hire additional workers at the going wage rate but find no more workers available at that rate*" (Nair, 1997).

The broad based and complete penetration of trade union activities is another feature that makes the rural labour market of the state distinct from the rest of India. The high degree of trade unionism, coupled with active state intervention has brought in a situation where the relationships and inter-linkages between the labour market with land and credit markets are rather weak or almost non-existent in the state. It is widely pointed out that, there has been a massive erosion of traditional labour relationships, as embodied in patron-client relationships. During the past few decades, several studies point out that the labour relations in rural Kerala are increasingly becoming formal and impersonal.

On the whole, rural labour market of Kerala is unique *vis-à-vis* its counterparts in the rest of India in terms of several aspects such as acute levels of unemployment, remarkably higher levels of nominal and real wages, increased levels of mobilisation and organisation of workers, impersonalisation and institutionalisation of employer-employee relations, and high penetration of state initiated redistributive and welfare measures.

The above macro-conceptualisations, however, could only provide a broad outline of the rural labour setting. In view of the considerable transformations in the overall economic and socio-political spheres in the state, there is a need to rethink the above generalizations. This becomes particularly relevant taking into account the temporal transformations in the agricultural development of the state. In recent decades, the state's economy has witnessed considerable transitions in its agricultural sector, with the prominence of small holding cultivation and visible changes in the cropping pattern. The pattern of land distribution and the nature of crops grown are the two key determinants of rural labour market dynamics. The drastic shift of the state's agrarian system from a seasonal and annual food crop cultivation regime to that of a tree crop based perennial farming system has argued to have brought in several changes in the labour requirements, which include numerous specificities in terms of skill and technology, along with rigidities in terms of labour absorption. The increased prominence of skill based agricultural operations (such as rubber tapping; coconut plucking) has also reported to lead to further segmentations in rural labour market.

The conceptualisation of rural labour markets based on the generic framework, thus, fails to fully explain the dynamics of rural labour market, characterised by the predominance of small holding cultivation and perennial tree crops. Given these structural changes in the state's economy in terms of pattern of land distribution and the nature of crops grown, there is a need for reconceptualising the existing macro understanding of the rural labour markets. Moreover, studies indicate that since 1980s, the Kerala labour lost its hegemony as a politically dictating group and its mass support. This downfall of the trade union movement would have implications on the labour relations across various segments of the rural labour market the details of which are yet to be explored and integrated to the macro-conceptualisations. All these caution towards the limitations of an arbitrary and universal application of macro-conceptualisations to all the sectors of the rural labour market. In this context, the present micro empirical study explores the labour issues and relations in the small holding sector of natural rubber plantations in Kerala.

Significance of Research on Rubber Holdings

Natural rubber cultivation plays a vital role in the rural economy of Kerala, accounting for 15.67 per cent of the total cropped area and 15.16 per cent of state's agricultural gross domestic product. The crop occupies second position next to coconut in terms of area with 4,75,039 hectares providing direct employment to more than 3.4 lakh persons per year (Rubber Board, 2000). The state holds a near monopoly position in the cultivation (84 per cent) and production (92 per cent) of natural rubber in India (Government of Kerala, 2003). An important feature of natural rubber economy of Kerala is the dominance of small holding sector, which accounts for more than 90 per cent of area under the crop. As per the classification followed by the Rubber Board, small holdings are those plots, which are less than 20 hectares (50 acres). Of late, it is widely understood that the small holding sector of natural rubber farming in Kerala exhibits marked differences in the labour tying arrangements and labour market characteristics, as opposed to the general agricultural scenario of the state and even to that of the estate sector (holdings of more than 20 hectares) of rubber plantations. The core parameters of labour contracts in the small holdings such as tenure of employment, wages, extra-wage and non-pecuniary benefits, terms of work, compensation provisions and so on are widely reported to vary drastically *vis-à-vis* those in the estate sector or rural/ agricultural sector as a whole. The small holdings are also characterised with piece rate wage payment system, which is quite different from the prominence of time rate payment systems in other agricultural sectors in general and in the organized estate sector of rubber plantations in particular. Further to this, there has been a growing apprehension that the terms and conditions of work and welfare aspects of rubber tappers in small holdings are strikingly unattractive compared to their counterparts in the estate sector.

As against the commonly accepted tendency of increasingly formal, impersonal and often-institutionalised employer-employee interactions in Kerala, with the massive erosion of the patron-client relations, the rubber holdings are mostly characterised with informal labour contracts, especially in tapping[13], which is the most important labour absorbing process in the natural rubber sector. The other distinct feature of small holdings is the lower degree of trade unionism, which is quite unanticipated in a state like Kerala, which has a fairly accredited history of working class struggles and trade union movement. The current state of organisational initiatives among the small holding tappers is at an alarmingly low level. With certain variations in the characterisation and features, the role of trade unions in workers' lives is reported to be extremely marginal, throughout the state. Preliminary observations suggest that the small holding rubber sector exhibits growing vulnerability of tappers with eroding bargaining powers and retention value of tappers. These tendencies are believed to have further accentuated during a prolonged crisis in the natural rubber sector since mid 1990s, due to the price slash on account of the integration of the domestic sector to the international markets.

From all these, it appears that the underlying features of labour relations in small holding rubber plantations is quite far and different from the macro-characteristics of the rural labour market of the state, which constitutes the premise of the study. The other reason for selecting small holding rubber plantations is the rather unexplored nature of labour relations and contractual arrangements in the sector. Further, the study also assumes relevance, as there is a felt need for approaching Kerala's labour market through the dynamics of small holding, tree-crop based and perennial cultivation, which has emerged as the important form of farming in the state.

Objectives and Methodology

The study aims at enriching the understanding of rural labour market dynamics of Kerala through capturing the specificities of labour relations in the small holding rubber sector. An attempt is made to integrate and contrast the specific characteristics of the sector to the overall rural labour situation in the state. More specifically, the study intends to:

(1) Conceptualise the broader characteristics and underlying paradoxes of rural labour market in the state;
(2) Explore the specific issues related to employment, wages and labour tying mechanisms in the small holding sector of natural rubber sector;
(3) Analyse the contractual arrangements and employment relations in the small holding sector; and
(4) Explore the livelihood diversification process of tappers and tapper households in the context of the crisis in the sector.

The study was carried out in three Taluks in Travancore-Cochin Region, the prominent belt of rubber cultivation in Kerala. These Taluks (Kanjirappally of Kottayam District, Nedumangad of Thiruvananthapuram District and Perumbavoor of Ernakulam District) were selected purposively considering two norms such as: vintage of the plantations and average size of holdings. Kanjirappally has a long history of rubber plantation (nearly 100 years) and is characterised with large-sized holdings. Nedumangad and Perumbavoor assume second and third positions respectively, in terms of plantation history (40-60 years and 20-40 years respectively) and size of holdings. The period of conducting the field study (2000-2002) also assumes importance as it coincides with the product market crisis in the rubber sector, which commenced in 1996 and is reported to have resulted in the deterioration of labour welfare and conditions of work.

The focus of the study is limited to tappers, who are engaged in the regular work of tapping—the most prominent labour absorbing activity in natural rubber holdings. A tapper is defined as a person who earns a major part of his/her income from tapping during the year preceding the survey. From each of the three selected areas, 120 tappers were surveyed. These tappers were found engaged in 595 plots. Apart from personal details of tappers, information was also collected on plot specific particulars, household details and livelihood strategies. Further to these, supplementary information was also gathered from several key resource persons including trade union leaders, social activists, officials from Rubber Board and Labour Department, rubber traders, elderly growers and other workers. The primary data is supplemented with available secondary information from various sources including Rubber Board and Panchayat Offices. Apart from these, to capture the macro picture of rural labour market in the state, relevant data is also drawn from secondary sources such as State Planning Board, NSSO and Rural Labour Enquiry Reports.

As the focus of the study is tappers, the findings are primarily based on the information provided by them, and thus may have an in built bias towards worker's perceptions. However, attempts are made to balance the findings through collecting supplementary information from select growers—20 each from the three study regions. Further, the findings of the study need to be understood in the specific context of declining prospects of tapping, on account of the continuing crisis in the rubber sector.

Scheme of the Book

The rest of the book is schemed as follows: Chapter 2 outlines the macro setting of the labour market in the state through an examination of the trends and patterns in employment and unemployment, temporal trends in rural labour, movements in rural wages. The chapter also discusses the dynamics of the rural labour market based on a detailed review of existing literature on the issue and posits some of the stylized facts. An attempt is made to provide an overview of the major theoretical approaches towards the conceptualisation of rural labour markets in Chapter 3, which also discusses the limitations in the acceptance of received general theories to explain the specific labour market conditions. The chapter also provides a brief account of the major empirical research on labour relations in rural areas, with a special focus on the developing country contexts. Chapter 4 elaborates the prominence of small holding sector in terms of area, production and employment as well as the labour process in tapping. It also gives detailed profile of the study areas and the methodology of data collection. Further, the chapter also explains the utility of engaging principal—agent theory as an analytical tool in understanding labour contracts in small holdings. The profile of respondents and conditions of work such as wages, employment and earnings are discussed in Chapter 5. The chapter also addresses the organisational and welfare related issues of tappers. Following this, Chapter 6 elaborates upon the various aspects of contractual arrangements in the small holdings and conceptualises the labour relations in the sector as an essential agency problem. The peculiar labour relations, which are socially embedded and based on personal ties, are found adversely affecting the bargaining power of tappers leading to deteriorating work conditions. Chapter 7 details out the income diversification process of tappers and tapper households and situate these survival strategies as an outcome of the declining prospects of the sector. Finally, Chapter 8 summarises the core findings of the study and situate the conclusions in the broader context of the state's rural labour market. The chapter also discusses certain policy implications.

APPENDIX

Table 1.1: Average Daily Wage Rates across Select Occupational Categories, Kerala and India, 2002-2003

Occupation	*Average Daily Wage Rate 2002-2003*		*% Difference from All India Average*
	Kerala	*India*	
Unskilled Labour			
Male	141.35	57.75	144.76
Female	99.28	43.42	128.66
Carpenter (Male)	190.32	105.81	79.87
Mason (Male)	183.89	116.34	58.06
Ploughing (Male)	242.95	71.53	239.65
Blacksmith (Male)	165.64	83.31	98.82
Well Digging (Male)	196.62	83.31	136.01
Sowing (Male)	173.28	62.62	176.72
Weeding (Female)	101.89	44.90	126.93
Transplanting (Female)	99.56	48.24	106.39
Harvesting (Female)	95.90	47.86	100.37

Source: Government of India, (2004).

NOTES

1. For a detailed discussion on the Kerala Model see Jeffrey (1992); Oommen (1999); and Parayil (2000).
2. It is widely observed that the radical reforms and redistributive measures followed by the various governments of Kerala are the prime factors that helped the state to achieve enviable levels of health, education and social justice (Franke and Chasin, 1997).
3. These enactments include, Kerala Agrarian Relations Act of 1960, Kerala Agricultural Workers' Act, 1975 and Kerala Land Reforms Amendment Act, 1979.
4. For detailed account of welfare funds see Waite, 2001 and Kannan, 2003.
5. "More than any other part of India in the early and mid-twentieth century, Kerala experienced the development of caste reform associations with extensive grass root participation and later on class based organisations such as trade unions and peasant movements. By the early 1950s, tens of thousands of rural and urban workers as well as tenant farmers and farm labourers were

experienced participants in petition and letter writing campaigns, street possessions, strikes and self help programmes such as reading rooms and village libraries" (Isaac *et al.*, 1998)

6. In the first few decades since the state's formation, all the governments in the state eventually followed a pro-worker stand. The cyclical trend in the coalition politics of the state forced the governments to recognise the worker organisations as powerful pressure groups. While portraying the collective political action of the workers, as a form of public action in deriving welfare outcomes, Ramachandran (1996) observes that: "government action in these spheres has been in response to political action by political parities of mass organisation of people". In a similar way, Heller (1995) view the agrarian transition of the state as follows: "While in rest of India, the agrarian transition was only piecemeal, mostly as a result of 'commercialisation of agriculture', in Kerala it was comprehensive and was at the behest of the mobilised working class".
7. "Intense political competition in a vigorous democratic system (an election every two years between 1948 and 1960) extracted programmes and services from governments desperate to win support to retain power. These programmes often worked relatively successfully because alert, literate consumers settled for nothing less. The outcome has been the Kerala Model—longer life, fewer infant deaths and a falling birth rate". (Jeffrey, 1992)
8. The land reforms introduced in Kerala in the early 1970s, abolishing tenancy, was the most successful among the land reforms in India.
9. For a detailed discussion on the issue see Tharamangalam (1998).
10. For a detailed discussion see Remesh (2003).
11. The hesitation of the unemployed to accept casual employment in rural areas and farm work and their stronger preference for selected jobs such as headload worker, shop assistant and so on could be viewed as a situation of a mismatch between the aspirations of youth and the available job opportunities.
12. Zacharia *et al.* (2002) estimate that the NRI remittances to Kerala were Rs. 12,110 crores in 1998; Rs. 14,143 crores in 1999; and Rs. 11,286 crores in 2000.
13. Tapping is the process of controlled wounding of the bark of the rubber tree to extract latex. It involves cutting open the latex vessels in the case of trees tapped for the first time or removing a thin shaving of bark with the coagula, which block the latex vessels in trees under regular tapping.

2

Labour Relations in Rural Kerala
An Overview

Many features of the labour market of Kerala are quite different from those of its counterparts in other parts of India, as discussed in Chapter 1. The state stands apart in many ways in terms of higher rate of unemployment (especially among educated); higher wages; better working conditions; effective protective cover (legislation and welfare programmes); and increasingly impersonal and formalised employer-employee relations. The departure of Kerala from the national pattern has been primarily attributed to the specific model of class formation and the institutional linkages that emerged from repeated cycles of class-based contestation and state intervention. The rural sector of the state is characterised by impersonal and institutionalised relations largely determined by the intervention of trade unions and the state, which is quite in contrast to the feudalistic and personalised relations seen in other parts of the country.

The present chapter provides the macro profile of human development as well as the labour market in the state and discusses the underlying dynamics of rural labour relations. The chapter is divided into 3 sections. Section 2.1 outlines the macro setting of the labour market in the state through an examination of the trends and patterns in employment and unemployment, temporal trends in rural labour, movements in rural wages. The subsequent section (2.2) discusses the dynamics of the rural labour market based on a detailed review of existing literature on the issue. The subsequent section (2.3) discusses the limitations of the existing macro generalisations of rural labour market and posits some of the stylized facts, which needs further examination.

The Macro Profile

On all the indicators of physical quality of life, Kerala far surpasses any Indian state and the performance of the state has been far above low-income countries, especially in the areas of health and education. As per 2001 Census, the literacy rate of the state is 90.9 per cent, compared to the national average of 65.4 per cent. Despite a lower per capita income compared to all India, the average Keralites can expect to live 12 years longer than the average Indian. The infant mortality rate of Kerala (14) is remarkably lower than that of all India (68). The state is also in an advanced stage of demographic transition with a visibly lower birth rates (17.9 as against all India rate of 25.8) and death rates (6.4 compared to 8.5 in all India). In terms of incidence of poverty also, Kerala's status is much higher than India, with a considerably lower proportion of the population falling below poverty line (18 per cent as against the all India average of 26 per cent) (Table 2.1).

Table 2.1: Comparison of Quality of Life Indicators: Kerala and India

Category	*Kerala*	*India*
Population (in millions) (2001)	31.8	102.7
Adult Literacy (per cent) (2001)		
Male	94.2	75.9
Female	87.9	54.1
Total	90.9	65.4
Life Expectancy at Birth (2001-2006)		
Male	71. 7	63.9
Female	75	66.9
Infant Mortality (per 1000 live births) (2000)		
Male	15	67
Female	13	69
Total	14	68
Adult Sex Ratio	1071	934
Birth Rate (per 1000) (2000)	17.9	25.8
Death Rate (per 1000) (2000)	6.4	8.5
Below Poverty Line (per cent) (2000)	18.0	26.1

Source: Government of India, *Economic Survey*, 2002-2003.

The state is also rated as more advanced in terms of standard indicators of women's status (e.g., literacy, health, demographic factors) than the rest of India. It is the only state in India with a sex ratio (i.e., the proportion of females to males) favourable to women. Apart from these favourable human development indicators, Kerala is also characterised by extensive network of roads, hospitals, educational institutions, and a wide system of public distribution outlets catering to the poorest groups, who are ordinarily cut off from the benefits of the market, owing to their lack of purchasing power (Isaac *et al.*, 1998).

Employment and Unemployment: Pattern and Trends

Kerala has the highest rates of unemployment in India, the degree of which had gone alarmingly high during the 1970s and the 1980s. The results of periodic surveys conducted by various government agencies and the data available with live registers of employment exchanges indicate that overall levels of unemployment in the state, especially among the educated youth, are on the rise. The states' performance in creating employment in public and industrial sectors has not been very successful, as many of the enterprises are running with heavy losses. The acute levels of unemployment, has been one of the crucial factors that intensified the economic crisis of the state since the late 1970s. The complexities of the labour market can be to a greater extent positioned and contextualised through a detailed understanding of the employment and unemployment situations in the state, which is attempted in the present subsection.

The Worker Population Ratios (WPR) in Kerala during 1971-2000 shows a visible and consistent decline since 1977-78 (Table 2.2). While the ratio for rural sector (UPSS) came down from 49.1 (in 1977-78) to 38.7 (in 1999-2000), that for urban sector during the same period came down from 43.9 to 37.3. A closer observation of the gender-wise components of ratios reveal that the overall decline was primarily due to the visible fall in participation rates of female population. Both in rural and urban areas, the ratios have declined drastically for female population, i.e., from 41.2 to 23.8 (in rural areas) and 32.5 to 20.3 (in urban areas). For males, it stood more or less unchanged over the period, while there was a slight decline in rural areas. The movements in the ratios of female worker population warrant a bit closer examination and explanation.

Table 2.2: Work Participation Rates in Kerala, 1971-1999/2000

Year	*Status*	*Rural*			*Urban*		
		Male	*Female*	*Total*	*Male*	*Female*	*Total*
1971	UPS	52.5	16.3	34.2	49.9	11.9	30.9
1972-73	UPSS	54.2	29.3	41.1	49.2	22.0	35.8
1977-78	UPSS	57.7	41.2	49.1	55.7	32.5	43.9
	UPS	49.4	21.1	34.7	49.4	15.5	32.1
1983	UPSS	55.2	35.0	44.7	55.6	24.3	39.2
	UPS	51.1	19.3	34.5	52.5	14.8	32.6
1987-88	UPSS	56.7	31.6	44.1	59.2	21.8	40.4
	UPS	52.6	19.5	36.0	55.0	15.0	34.9
1993-94	UPSS	53.7	23.8	38.1	55.9	20.3	37.7
	UPS	51.5	15.2	32.5	54.2	15.2	34.2
1999-	UPSS	55.3	23.8	38.7	55.8	20.3	37.3
2000	UPS	52.6	15.9	33.3	53.4	15.6	33.7

Source: NSSO, Various Rounds
Note: UPS: Usual Principal Status
UPSS: Usual Principal and Subsidiary Status

The participation ratio of female population in rural Kerala has come down; whatsoever may be the status under consideration (UPS or UPSS). This decline in participation rate for females could be attributed to the decline in traditional industries like cashew and coir. Other possible reasons include: (a) the drastic decline in area under paddy cultivation, which is a prime source of women's work in the rural areas; and (b) increased enrolment of girl children in schools and prolonged years of education of female students as against the situation in the 1970s. The WPR for females in the urban areas shows a slightly different picture. When we consider only the principal status of female population, the ratio remained more or less unchanged. However, the inclusion of subsidiary employment makes the scene different. During 1977-78 to 1999-2000, the proportion declined from 32.5 per cent to 20.3 per cent, clearly indicating the withdrawal of women from subsidiary employment. One major reason for this may be the increased level of education of females, which naturally reflects in a decline of subsidiary activities.

The other important issue is the stagnation of urban female participation in principal employment status, over the years. One of the reasons which could probably explain the situation is the marked increase in migration of educated, skilled or semi-skilled women workers to other states within India and abroad, for purpose of employment.

A comparison of age specific WPR between Kerala and All India, according to UPS and UPSS shows that maximum number of workers in the state is of the age group 35-50, with increased concentration in the group 40-44 (Table 2.3). Thus, it

Table 2.3: Age Specific Work Participation Rates (UPS and UPSS) for Kerala and All India

Category	*Age Group (Years)*													
	0-4	*5-9*	*10-14*	*15-19*	*20-24*	*25-29*	*30-34*	*35-39*	*40-44*	*45-49*	*50-54*	*55-59*	*60 and above*	*All*
Kerala														
Rural														
UPS	0.2	0	0.3	17.5	41.5	50.3	56.8	61.9	61.2	61.8	58.0	47.6	27.2	33.3
UPSS	—	0	0.7	19.6	45.9	57.5	65.4	69.9	73.0	70.1	63.9	61.5	36.3	38.7
Urban														
UPS	—	0	0.3	12.2	33.3	54.9	56.8	61.3	65.7	61.1	63.5	45.6	24.0	33.7
UPSS	—	0	0.5	14.9	36.9	57.6	60.2	67.2	70.9	67.3	68.9	52.0	31.7	37.3
India														
Rural														
UPS	—	0.6	7.8	36.4	55.7	64.8	68.7	72.0	73.0	72.3	68.3	63.4	39.9	38.0
UPSS	—	0.7	9.3	41.1	61.8	71.3	75.8	78.4	79.1	78.0	74.1	68.8	43.0	41.7
Urban														
UPS	—	0.2	3.8	20.4	40.1	52.4	58.0	61.1	64.5	62.9	61.6	50.2	22.7	32.4
UPSS	—	0.3	4.3	21.8	42.0	54.3	59.9	63.7	66.4	64.5	63.3	51.7	24.1	33.7

Source: NSSO 55th Round (2000).

Note: UPS: Usual Principal Status.
UPSS: Usual Principal and Subsidiary Status.

shows that there is not much difference between Kerala and All India in terms of the modal age group of worker participation. In All India also, 40-44 is the age group of participation of the workers. Both in rural and urban areas, engagement of children below age 15 is minimal in Kerala, compared to rest of India.

The data shows that in the case of urban areas, the WPR in Kerala is slightly higher than that of All India while in the case of rural areas, it is significantly lower than the national ratio. The participation rate of elderly (above 60 years) is higher for the urban areas of Kerala, than All India. The pattern is reverse in the case of rural areas. The participation rate at higher ages in the urban areas may be due to increased opportunities for employment coupled with the high life expectancy.

The industry-wise distribution of employment shows that agriculture, manufacturing, trade and community services are the industries in which rural population mainly works (Table 2.4). In urban areas too, the above said categories, except agriculture, are prominent in providing employment. In general, agriculture continues to be the most important activity

Table 2.4: Distribution of Usually Employed Persons by Industry, 1999-2000 (per cent)

Industry	*UPSS*				*UPS*			
	Kerala		*All India*		*Kerala*		*All India*	
	Rural	*Urban*	*Rural*	*Urban*	*Rural*	*Urban*	*Rural*	*Urban*
Agriculture	48.3	9.5	76.3	8.8	42.3	7.1	75.1	7.9
Mining and Quarrying	1.7	0.3	0.5	0.8	1.9	0.4	0.5	0.8
Manufacturing	12.6	20.2	7.4	22.7	13.5	21.7	7.4	22.6
Electricity	0.2	0.5	0.2	0.7	0.2	0.6	0.2	0.7
Construction	9.4	10.7	3.3	8.0	10.7	11.7	3.5	8.2
Whole Sale/ Retail Trade etc.	11.9	30.5	5.1	26.9	13.5	28.3	5.4	27.0
Transport, Storage etc.	6.2	8.7	2.1	8.7	7.0	9.5	2.3	9.0
Financial, Insurance Services etc.	1.8	4.4	0.3	4.1	2.0	4.7	0.4	4.1
Community Services	8.1	15.2	4.9	19.5	8.9	16.0	5.2	19.7
All	100	100	100	100	100	100	100	100

Source: NSSO 55th Round (2000).

that absorbs labour force in the state. However, there is a visible rural-urban distinction in terms of prominence of agriculture. Both in rural and urban areas, the shares of service sector are significant in employment. While about half of the (48.3 per cent) rural population is dependent on agriculture in rural areas, it is only less than one tenth (9.5 per cent) in urban Kerala.

The data reveals the prominence of agriculture in rural areas is more pronounced at the All India level (with more than 75 per cent of the workers engaged in the sector as against the 40-50 per cent in the case of Kerala) irrespective of their employment status. All industries, except agriculture and electricity, in Kerala show larger number of worker participation as compared to All-India in the rural areas. In urban areas, the prominence of agriculture is slightly more in Kerala.

Distribution of the workforce according to the nature of employment—self-employed, regular employed and casual labour—provides better insights on the composition of the labour market. The data shows that casual labour assumes the prime category in rural Kerala, whatsoever may be the status of work under consideration (Table 2.5). Regular employment is the less pronounced category in rural areas, while it is equally prominent as that of casual labour in urban areas. Self-employment, the second major category that provides living to more than one-third of workers both in urban and rural areas.

Table 2.5: Distribution of Usually Employed Persons by Status of Employment, 1999-2000 (per cent)

Category	*UPS*			*UPSS*		
	Self Employed	*Regular/ salaried*	*Casual Labour*	*Self Employed*	*Regular/ salaried*	*Casual Labour*
Kerala						
Rural	35.4	15.8	48.8	42.9	13.7	43.4
Urban	36.4	31.8	31.8	41.3	29.1	29.6
India						
Rural	53.1	7.5	39.4	55.8	6.8	37.4
Urban	40.7	41.3	18.0	42.2	40.0	17.8

Source: NSSO 55th Round (2000).

The incidence of casual labour is high in Kerala compared to the All India average, irrespective of whether one considers subsidiary activity or not. This is true for both urban and rural areas. The regular employed workers in rural areas are much higher than the All India average. Compared to All India averages, the participation of self-employed workers is low in Kerala, though self-employment assumes an important share in total population in the state. This may be because of the higher degree of regular employment in rural areas.

One of the striking aspects of unemployment in the state is its increase in 1999-2000 after a spell of decline till 1993-94 (Table 2.6). Unemployment rates, irrespective of the statuses, show an increase during 1999-2000 for rural areas for both male and females. The trend is true for urban area also, except for male in the UPS and UPSS statuses.

Table 2.6: Unemployment Rates in Kerala, 1977-78 to 1999-2000

Year	*UPS*			*UPSS*			*CWS*			*CDS*		
	M	F	P	M	F	P	M	F	P	M	F	P
1977-78												
Rural	13.5	29.2	19.2	4.7	7.6	6	12.2	12.8	12.4	25	27.4	25.8
Urban	16.2	39.5	23.5	8.5	16.5	11.7	15.1	14.7	15	25	25.5	25.1
1983												
Rural	10.6	17	12.6	7	7.2	7.1	13.4	5.2	5.2	24.3	31.1	26.2
Urban	11.9	25.6	15.6	9.4	19.4	11.4	13.9	16.3	16.3	22.7	29	24.3
1987-88												
Rural	12.5	25	16.6	9.3	14.9	11.5	14.4	17.2	17.2	16.7	27.4	20
Urban	14.1	33.8	19.6	10.2	24.1	14.5	14.5	19.5	19.5	22.4	40.3	27.1
1993-94												
Rural	7.2	15.8	9.4	5.5	9.7	6.9	7.1	8.9	8.9	13.1	19	14.7
Urban	6.6	24.4	12	6.6	18.7	10.3	9.3	12.9	12.9	14.1	27.8	17.7
1999-2000												
Rural	7.6	19.7	10.9	5.7	13	8.2	10.1	12.5	12.5	20	26.1	21.7
Urban	6.9	26.4	12.5	5.6	20	10.2	9.7	13.8	13.8	15.5	28.2	19.1

Source: NSSO, Various Rounds.
Note: UPS: Usual Principal Status.
UPSS: Usual Principal and Subsidiary Status.
CWS: Current Weekly Status.
CDS: Current Daily Status.

From the foregoing discussion, it is evident that there exist sharp differences in employment and unemployment trends across rural and urban areas. Further, it is suggestive of the continuing centrality of rural sector in the employment scene, given the limited scope for expansion of gainful employment opportunities in the industrial and urban sectors. In this backdrop, the subsequent discussions in the section focuses on the specific trends and patterns in rural labour households and overall movement of wages, which is a central parameter in the understanding of rural labour dynamics.

Trends in Rural Labour Households

A distinction of 'rural ' and 'urban' workers (based on official criteria involving demographic and other factors) is all the more indefensible in the case of Kerala, because of the absence of any sharp differences between rural and urban areas. The adjective 'rural' brings to the fore that stratum of the workers, which is linked to agriculture and rural industry through land and other natural resources and its concomitant exploitation. By rural working class, it is meant that the set of agricultural labour, plantation workers and other workers in a variety of rural industries.

Rural labour households[1] constitute for about 47 per cent of total rural household in 1999-2000 (Table 2.7) in Kerala, one of the highest figures for any state in India (40.2 per cent is the All India figure). The share of rural labour households in all rural households has increased till 1983, after which there is a trend of decline.

The share of agricultural labour households has shown a decline except for 1983 where it stood at 64.3 per cent. During the period 1987-88 and 1999-2000 the share has considerably dipped to 46.9 per cent indicating the growing prominence of non-farm employment in rural areas of the state.

Table 2.7: Estimated Number of Rural Labour Households by Classes of Households 1964-65 to 1999-00 (000s)

Year	*Rural HHs*	*Rural lab HHs*	*Percentage of rural labour HHs in rural HHs*	*Agri. Labour HHs*	*Percentage of labour HHs to rural labour HHs*
1964-65	2475	1041	42.0	697	67.0
1974-75	3234	1364	42.2	886	65.0
1977-78	3816	1809	47.4	1030	57.0
1983	3622	1785	49.3	1148	64.3
1987-88	3912	1872	47.9	1179	63.0
1993-94	3905	1866	47. 8	1102	59.1
1999-00	4437	2066	46. 6	969	46.9

Source: RLE Report, Various Volumes.

The percentage share of agricultural labour to total labour in the rural labour households has almost remained constant till 1983 but has shown a drastic decline since then (Table 2.8). During 1993/94-1999/2000 the share has dipped by almost 30 per cent, which further confirms the significance of rural non-farm sector. With the growing prominence of non-farm sector in the rural areas, it is important to examine how the rural wages reflect the changed scenario. Accordingly, the subsequent session discusses the trends, patterns and inter-linkages in rural wages in Kerala since 1980s.

Table 2.8: Estimated Number of Agricultural and Non-agricultural Labour in all Rural Households 1964-65 to 1999-00 (000s)

Year	*Agri. labour*	*Non-agri. labour*	*Total labour*	*Agri. labour as per cent of total labour*
1964-65	1351	658	2009	67.3
1974-75	1860	937	2797	66.5
1977-78	1909	936	2845	67.1
1983	1808	854	2662	67.9
1987-88	1307	834	2141	61.1
1993-94	736	626	1362	54.0
1999-00	1420	1543	2963	47.9

Source: RLE Report, Various Volumes.

Trends and Patterns in Rural Wages

The state of Kerala has always been a high wage region, especially in terms of rural wages. A comparison of average daily wages of casual workers for rural areas with the national average and that of Tamil Nadu suggests that the rural wages in the state are more than double compared to the All India figure and considerably high even compared to the neighbouring state (Table 2.9).

Table 2.9: Comparison of Average Daily Wages of Casual Workers in Rural Areas; 1999-2000 at current prices (Rs.)

State	*Male*	*Female*	*Persons*
Kerala	100. 8	56.7	90.6
Tamil Nadu	60.2	30.8	48.1
India	44.8	29.0	39.6

Source: NSSO 55th Round, 2000.

The temporal variations in rural wages during the period 1980-81 to 2001-02 have been captured using the data provided by the Department of Economics and Statistics, Government of Kerala. The analysis is attempted for six prominent categories of rural labour such as male paddy field worker, female paddy field worker, carpenter, mason, male unskilled worker and female unskilled worker.

In the cases of the two prominent skilled occupations in the rural sector such as mason and carpenter, the nominal wages show continuous increases over the period. However, their respective annual rates of change have come down drastically from their peak of 22 and 23 per cent in 1995-96 to 3 per cent each in 2001-02. For the past few years, the rates of change have been continuously on the decline. The nominal wage rates of paddy workers (both male and female) have also shown increases over the period, but with drastic declines in the rates of change since the mid 1990s. Similar patterns are visible in the cases of unskilled workers, both male and female, though the declines in the rate of growth show a lag of around two-three years (Table 2.10).

Table 2.10: Average Daily Wage Rates Across Categories of Rural Workers (in Rs.)

Year	Skilled Workers in Rural Sector				Paddy Field Workers				Unskilled Workers in Construction			
	Average Daily Wage Rates		% change previous year		Average Daily Wage Rates		% change previous year		Average Daily Wage Rates		% change previous year	
	Carpenter	Mason	Carpenter	Mason	Male	Female	Male	Female	Male	Female	Male	Female
1980-81	20	20	—	—	11	8	—	—	12	10	—	—
1981-82	22	23	13	14	13	9	14	12	15	11	24	19
1982-83	23	24	4	5	13	10	4	8	18	14	17	19
1983-84	26	26	12	11	16	11	19	16	20	15	14	9
1984-85	39	39	48	48	24	12	49	8	22	16	8	11
1985-86	43	43	11	21	26	15	11	27	25	19	16	17
1986-87	46	45	7	7	28	16	9	9	28	21	9	10
1987-88	48	47	3	3	30	16	7	8	31	23	13	11
1988-89	50	50	5	5	32	19	5	5	33	25	5	9
1989-90	52	51	4	4	33	20	4	6	34	27	4	6
1990-91	54	54	5	5	36	21	7	8	37	29	9	9
1991-92	59	59	8	8	41	26	15	24	40	32	6	8
1992-93	68	68	16	16	48	32	17	24	46	37	17	18
1993-94	76	77	12	13	54	35	12	10	50	41	9	10
1994-95	87	87	14	14	64	42	17	18	60	50	19	22
1995-96	107	106	23	22	77	51	21	22	77	63	27	26
1996-97	129	128	20	21	92	61	19	18	88	74	16	17
1997-98	146	144	14	13	104	69	13	15	101	85	15	15
1998-99	155	155	7	7	112	71	8	3	111	93	10	10
1999-2000	165	165	6	6	119	79	6	10	125	103	13	10
2000-2001	177	175	6	6	126	85	6	8	129	106	3	3
2001-2002	182	180	3	3	127	89	1	4	130	110	1	4

Source: Department of Economics and Statistics, Government of Kerala collated in *Economic Review*, State Planning Board, Various Issues.

What do these trends suggest? Though there have been continuous gains in nominal wages across all occupations, the rates of increase have drastically come down since mid 1990s and there is a tendency towards, further reduction in the rate of change. In other words, the data is indicative of a possible stagnancy or reduction of nominal wages in the coming years.

Given the drastic decline in the rates of change of nominal wage rates, it is also imperative to examine the movements in real wages over the period. Accordingly, real wages have been calculated for all the six categories of occupations by deflating the nominal wages by the consumer price indices provided by the Labour Bureau for the agricultural labourers (Table 2.11).

Table 2.11: Daily Real Wage Movements Across Rural Occupations

Base year 1960-61 =100

Years	*Daily Real Wage Rates (Rs.)*					
			Paddy Field Workers		*Unskilled Workers in Construction*	
	Carpenter	*Mason*	*Male*	*Female*	*Male*	*Female*
1980-81	5.5	5.5	3.1	2.2	3.4	2.7
1981-82	5.6	5.6	3.2	2.2	3.8	2.8
1982-83	5.3	5.4	3.0	2.2	4.1	3.1
1983-84	4.9	4.9	3.0	2.1	3.8	2.8
1984-85	6.4	6.4	3.9	2.0	3.6	2.7
1985-86	7.4	7.4	4.5	2.6	4.4	3.3
1986-87	7.2	7.2	4.5	2.6	4.4	3.3
1987-88	6.9	6.9	4.4	2.4	4.6	3.4
1988-89	6.8	6.7	4.3	2.5	4.5	3.4
1989-90	6.1	6.1	3.9	2.3	4.0	3.2
1990-91	5.8	5.7	3.8	2.3	4.0	3.1
1991-92	5.7	5.6	4.0	2.5	3.8	3.0
1992-93	5.9	5.8	4.2	2.8	4.0	3.2
1993-94	5.8	5.8	4.1	2.7	3.8	3.1
1994-95	6.0	6.0	4.3	2.9	4.1	3.4
1995-96	6.5	6.4	4.7	3.1	4.6	3.8
1996-97	7.0	6.9	5.0	3.3	4.8	4.0
1997-98	7.6	7.5	5.4	3.6	5.3	4.4
1998-99	7.8	7.7	5.6	3.6	5.5	4.7
1999-2000	8.1	8.0	5.8	3.8	6.1	5.0
2000-2001	8.4	8.3	6.0	4.1	6.1	5.0
2001-2002	8.6	8.5	6.0	4.2	6.2	5.2

Source: Calculated from data of Department of Economics and Statistics, Government of Kerala—collated in *Economic Review*, State Planning Board, Various Issues.

The real wage estimates suggest continous marginal increases, in all the select rural occupations. Though there have been some indications towards a stagnating real wage trends, since early 2000, it is premature to arrive at some definite conclusions. Overall, the data shows a strong case of wage rigidity in the downward direction.

The pattern in wage movements also suggests a broad tendency of wages in different categories to move in a more or less same direction in rural Kerala (Figures 2.1 and 2.2). This is indicative of an interrelated wage structure in the rural economy where one category of the rural wage might be influenced or related to other wages in the system[2].

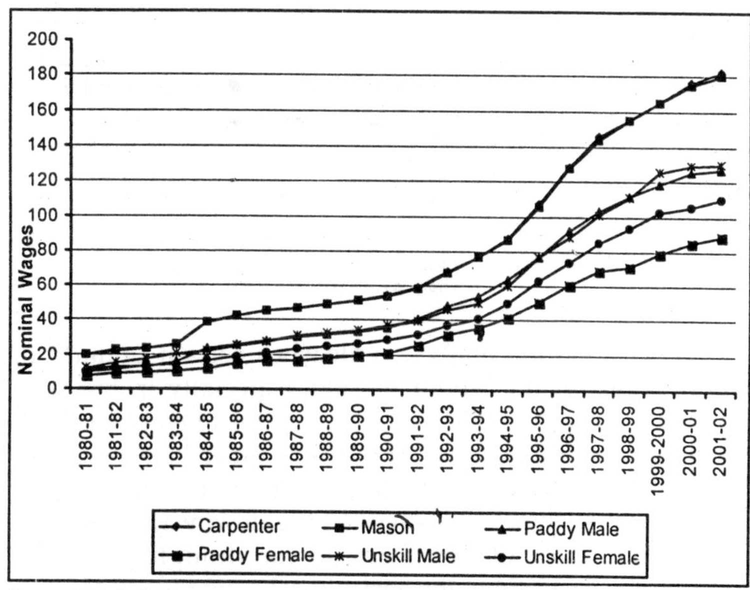

Source: Table 2.10

Fig. 2.1: Relative Movements of Nominal Wages in Rural Kerala, 1980/81-2001/02

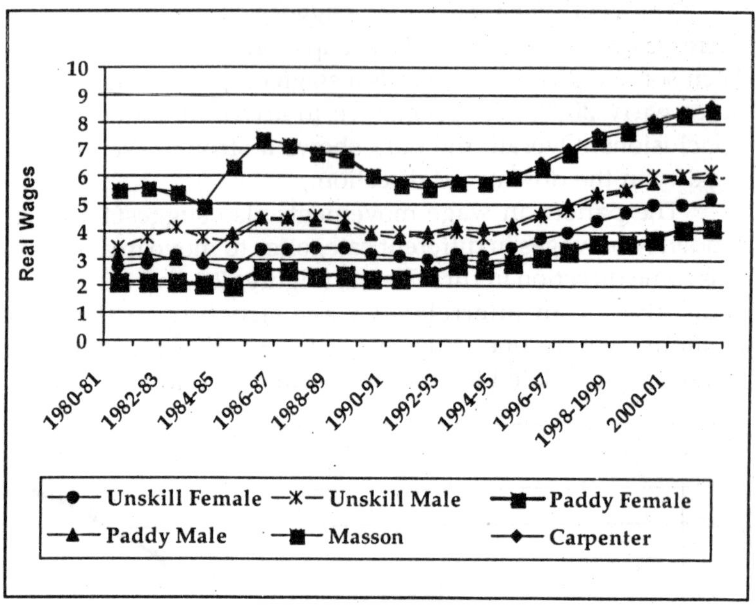

Source: Table 2.11

Fig. 2.2: Relative Movements of Real Wages in Rural Kerala, 1980/81-2001/02

The foregoing analysis unleashes certain underlying complexities in the labour market, especially in the rural segment, of the state. On the one hand, the unemployment is alarmingly on the increase. At the same time, the wages (both nominal and real) have not suffered yet, indicating a strong tendency of stickiness of wages in the downward direction. The prominence of non-farm sector though increased considerably over time, the agricultural activities continue to be the prime source of employment among the rural labour households. Further, the relative position of agricultural wages in the overall rural wage hierarchy has shown considerable levels of stability. These complexities and paradoxes in the labour market have been subjects of analysis and debates, especially in the context of the overall development discourse of the state. The subsequent section provides an overview of the major discourses on labour market based on the existing literature on the subject, with special emphasis on rural labour relations.

Labour Market Dynamics: A Discussion

A closer examination of the Kerala's labour market discloses two dilemmas underlying its dynamics such as a perceived mismatch between labour supply and demand and the coexistence of higher levels of unemployment alongside high wages. These paradoxes are seen as outcomes of specific patterns of class formation and institutional linkages that characterise the state's development trajectory.

The emergence of a market for rural labour in the state is closely related to the commercialisation of agriculture. The extent as well as the growth of wage labour in rural Kerala is quite high compared to other states in India. The early and sustained penetration of capitalism in agro based rural industry has played a major role in the spread of wage labour. Further, the relatively high growth of population during the past century also increased the pressure on land. With the commercialization of agriculture, the traditional labour institution under the caste system based on social stratification gave way to the emergence of wage labour.

As discussed in Chapter 1, due to the cumulative effects of several historical factors, trade unions have emerged as powerful institutions in the state over a long period of time. Two features specific to the ecological situation of Kerala, have favoured the mobilisation and organisation of rural workers. The first is the spatial concentration of large groups of workers as a result of specialisation and export of a variety of commercial crops and their processing as rural industrial activities. The second is the absence of sharp distinction between rural and urban areas. Thus, while workers movement was initially confined to the tiny urban surroundings, the need to expand the mass base of the movement led to incorporation of large number of rural workers. The rural urban continuum of Kerala's spatial ordering has further facilitated the integration of workforce.

Kerala witnessed an early mobilisation of a large segment of the traditional labour force, which was the cumulative outcome of a host of factors including the social reform movements, nationalist politics accompanied by radical political movement and a strong labour welfare oriented government. Trade unions were formed not only among agricultural, industrial and public service employees, but also in the informal labour sector.

The other important factor that has shaped the labour market in Kerala is the extensive state intervention. The relationship between working class mobilisation and Kerala's achievement on the social front is well documented. The direct interventions such as the land reforms and minimum wage legislation have led to the enhancement of reservation wages and thus increased bargaining power of the working class. Landlessness is very low among rural labour households with majority owning some land as a result of land reforms in the state. Under the land reforms, agricultural and other rural labour households who had no land of their own but those who were residing on the land owned by landowners were given 10 cents of land per household as homestead land. The consequence of the land ownership programme, howsoever small the plot size has been that only a small percentage of the agricultural labour households in the state have remained land less. In 1959, one third of the rural households did not own any land. By 1980s, 92.2 per cent of the rural labour households owned land in the state (Oommen 1999, Lieten, 2002). Under Kerala's ecological conditions of rainfall, soil fertility and the density of population, homesteads are cultivated with few coconut trees, bananas and some root crops. Since such land are treated as cultivated, majority of rural labour households come under the category of those who own agricultural land.

The main impact of minimum wage legislation in the state has been an increase in the bargaining power and the consequent reduction in the authority of the employers. The state also took considerable initiatives in the formation of labour co-operatives[3] and setting up of welfare boards[4]. The social legislations and pro-labour movements have provided the working class with an exceptionally high degree of bargaining capacity, which is more visible in the unorganised sector. The efforts of unions and state agencies in Kerala have combined to penetrate effectively the unorganised or informal economy drawing large chunk of traditionally disenfranchised workers within the purview of law and the protection of the social welfare state (Heller, 1999).

Indirect state intervention comprises of various consumption subsidising programmes such as PDS and other welfare schemes for the weaker sections. The broad based redistributive measures followed by various governments has provided the general population with more equitable access to basic goods including education, health service and subsidised food, thereby leading to higher levels of social and human development. This has enhanced the purchasing power as well as the bargaining power of labour.

These developments have necessitated institutionalisation and impersonalisation of labour relations even in the rural and informal sectors leading to the erosion of traditional labour relations as embodied in patron-client relationships and the interlinkage between land, labour and credit markets. The unionisation and state intervention have transformed the traditional character of labour relations and facilitated the introduction of new institutional mechanisms of wage determination through collective bargaining. It is also widely pointed out that the protective social legislation and horizontal mobilisation have supplanted patron-client and despotic relations of employment in rural Kerala with more formal, impersonal and contractual ones. The broad based presence of trade unions in the rural set up, has given rise to the existence of higher wage rates, which do not significantly vary with seasons and across localities. The importance of trade unions of Kerala in maintaining a higher wage rate in the labour market is a widely accepted fact. It is often observed that trade union movements do not permit workers to offer their labour power at lower wages, even when unemployed (Krishnan, 1991).

All these developments resulted in the erosion of interlinkages between land, labour and credit markets. Labour relations in the state's rural set up are widely understood as increasingly impersonal, though to a limited extent, they retain the basic characteristics of stratification and segmentation embedded in the traditional social order. Here, the stratification is related to the hierarchy of occupations depending upon the nature of the job, earnings and security whereas segmentation refers to the boundaries existing within a given stratum of labour market. The main sources of these features lie in the institution of caste considerations.

The combined impact of all these has been a felt rigidity in the supply of labour. The caste composition of labour households has important implications for labour supply. Traditionally, a substantial proportion of rural labour, more particularly agriculture labour has been coming from the scheduled caste communities. Several studies have documented that the implementation of land reforms in the state has bestowed on the members of *Harijan* communities a homestead and a few cents of garden land, and thereby negatively affecting the labour supply. Further, the access to land has reported to have restricted the mobility of the erstwhile landless labour significantly leading to a visible decline in inter-village mobility of workers.

Another reason for the rigidities in the labour market is the spread of education. It is widely noted by researchers that the higher education status of the state has adversely affected the labour market as educated youngsters regard 'blue collar jobs' inferior. The high literacy rate also implies that sizeable proportion of the lower age group is kept out of the work force as students, who constitute a substantive segment of the non-workers.

Yet another factor, which has contributed to the increased reservation price of labour, is the large-scale migration, especially to middle east. Since the mid 1970s onwards, the acute levels of unemployment has induced many Keralites to migrate to the countries of middle east. This massive exodus and subsequent inflow of remittances resulted in far reaching transformation in the living standards of workers, increasing the reservation income of other members of such households.

The increased levels of household resource base, through remittances, have also enabled some youngsters to make their choice of not to work manually but to wait until they get some white-collar jobs. The development of a strong non-agricultural labour market has also influenced the setting of the labour market. The 'construction boom' as a result of large inflow of remittances from the Middle East since mid the 1970s enhanced the opportunities for unskilled workers. This increased the wages of non-agricultural labour, reducing the supply of labour in the farming sector.

The other major concern in the rural sector is the mismatch between supply of and demand for labour. When it is widely acknowledged that the rural unemployment, especially those of educated youths, is on the rise in the state, there are several sectors in the rural labour market that report acute levels of labour shortage. Nevertheless, the excess supply of labour or shortage of labour is not uniform across occupations, but is fragmented by skill (Nair, 1997). The higher social development of the rural population, especially the younger age group, is found to have given rise to a change in expectations with respect to nature and duration of employment. The educated younger generation expects more regular and clean jobs as opposed to the casual employment in agriculture and rural industries involving drudgery and low social status. It is widely acknowledged in the literature that there is a noticeable hesitation among the unemployed to employment in agriculture. A definite pattern of shift of workforce from agriculture to non-farm sectors has also been acknowledged (Mahesh, 2002). Further, it is observed that the educated youth are not available for farm work, despite being unemployed. This selective preference of educated unemployed has resulted in the emergence of a vast reservoir of job seekers amidst labour shortages for unskilled manual labour on a casual basis. Pursuit of higher qualification has been yet another mechanism of adjustment during the waiting period for desired formal sector employment. Here the pursuit of higher qualification tends to increase the probability of getting some employment, even if it is non-commensurate with the qualification. This *inter alia* leads to another paradox of continued demand for degrees despite high unemployment among educated (Isaac and Tharakan, 1995).

The tendency of disdaining manual work could be seen more as a 'social stigma', which itself raises several other issues. There is a growing consensus that the massive spread of education, during a period social transformation and increased opening up of the economy (especially through emigration towards gulf countries) have altered the aspirations of the job seeking youth in rural Kerala. Thus, the paradox could be situated as more 'social' where mismatch is actually between the aspirations of youth and the available job opportunities. Even with the aversion towards agricultural work, it has been documented that there exists a strong preference among the youngsters for selected manual jobs as head load worker; shop assistant and so on. This led to an inference that the aversion of Kerala youth is mainly towards casual employment in rural areas and farm work. The tendency is so strong that even when they are unemployed, farm work is not reckoned as a desirable option among the youngsters in rural area. Younger members of rural labour households are reported to show strong preference towards service sector jobs and thus are ready to wait until they secure such employment. However, it has been observed that due to prolonged waiting period involved in getting their perceived reserved job status, many educated unemployed tend to seek employment in new informal sectors which offer no security or fair wage but are nearer to their aspired job status (Isaac and Tharakan, 1995).

Blocking of technological change in productive sectors by trade unions has also found to have resulted in the massive flight of capital from the state to neighbouring states, thus affecting the employment. Further to this, the gaining of a militant image in the labour front, during 1970s and 1980s, is also highlighted to have blocked the inflow of private capital into the state. High wages, state enforced controls on mechanisation; rigidities in labour deployment and high levels of social consumption are argued to have contributed to either driving capital away or creating significant barriers to internal capital accumulation. In this context, it has been observed that though broad trade unionism and worker mobilisation in the state, though succeeded in bringing out higher levels of wages, resulted in massive erosion of job opportunities leading to increased levels of rural unemployment in the long run. The stronger aversion, among youngsters, towards manual work and the increased preference for white collar work are argued to have led to the influx of workers from neighbouring states to fill manual jobs that Keralites prefer not to occupy (Waite, 2001). For instance, it is estimated that over a million manual labour have migrated to Kerala from Tamil Nadu and Andhra Pradesh in recent years to fill shortages in agricultural and construction markets (Parameswaran, 1998).

In agriculture, the higher wage rates have resulted in a continous increase in the cost of cultivation of labour intensive crops such as paddy, which in turn has led to a host of crop substitution strategies. As a result of this, the cropping pattern in the state has witnessed a significant shift from labour intensive seasonal food crops to less labour demanding perennial cash crops during the past three decades. Rice and tapioca the two most important food crops in Kerala, together constituted around 40 per cent of the total cropped area in 1970s. The proportion has dropped to less than 20 per cent by 2000. On the other hand, the proportion of area under coconut and rubber has increased from 30 per cent to 45 per cent during this period. In rural industries, such as cashew and coir, the rise in wages led to a situation of migration of capital to low wage areas in neighbouring states where the organized power of labour is weak (Government of Kerala, 2001).

The forgoing discussion, helps in delineating some of the major macro characteristics of the Kerala's rural labour market, such as: (a) high degree of unionisation among workers; (b) existence of comparatively higher level of wages, along with extreme downward rigidity; (c) higher reservation price of labour; (d) aversion towards agricultural work and strong preference for service sector employment; (e) highly impersonal and institutionalised employer—employee relations; and (f) segmentation of labour market by skill and type of tasks.

Rethinking Generalisations and Revisiting Stylized Facts

Of late, there is a growing realisation that, the above macro characteristics could be relied on only for arriving at a broader conceptualisation of the state's rural labour market. It is cautioned by many scholars that the universal application of these features to all the segments of the rural sector may be misleading as these features could at best be treated only as 'central tendencies' (Kurien 2000; Lindberg, 2001).

An important limitation of the existing theorisation of rural labour market of Kerala is its excessive emphasis on labour relations in large-scale annual crop farming, especially paddy. Of the several factors that influence the demand for labour the two closely connected and widely acknowledged are the land distribution pattern and cropping pattern. The agricultural sector in the state is characterised by small holding cultivation with more than 80 per cent of the agricultural holdings below half a hectare in size. Thus, land distribution is less skewed and most of the labour possesses some land. Most of the cultivation is carried out in small and scattered homestead farms where the average size of agricultural holdings is below 30 cents (Isaac and Tharakan, 1995). This comparatively equitable distribution of land is often overseen by most of the researchers.

Further, the agricultural sector of the state has been undergoing a structural transformation since 1970s with large-scale shift of cultivation from seasonal and annual food crops to perennial cash crops. This has resulted in the pre-dominance of commercial and perennial tree crops in the agrarian economy, which has important implications for the demand for labour. The seasonal crops create peak labour demand during planting and harvesting seasons. In the intervening period also some labour is required for the maintenance of the crops. The demand for labour, thus, is high but seasonal. Perennial crops generate more demand for labour during the initial years. Once the trees are grown, only lesser quantum of labour is required mostly for maintenance and harvest. As the tasks associated with tree crops are not season specific, it helps to wipe offs the large gaps in labour absorption between the peak and off seasons. The labour demand in a perennial crop regime to a greater extent is related to the age structure of the trees. Further, most of the tasks associated with the harvesting and maintenance of tree crops are highly skilled and specialised and hence the labour market is segmented. Nair (1997) argues that there exists a situation of relative labour shortage caused by small holder tree crop character due to imperfections and segmentation of the rural labour market. This predominance of small holder tree crop character of the agricultural sector, accompanied by high transaction costs due to various imperfections and segmentation of labour market is argued to be one of the major reasons for the paradoxes and riddles in the state's rural labour market in the recent decades. The radical changes in Kerala's agrarian economy have also led to transformations in the nature of agricultural activities and status of employment of cultivators. A substantial number of agricultural families have non-agricultural sources of income. This increased prevalence of part time cultivation has resulted in a situation where the average farmer in the state could be characterised as a 'gentle man farmer' who is not personally engaged in most of the agricultural operations (Tharamangalam, 1998).

The later half of the 1990s also witnessed a crisis in the rural sector of Kerala, owing to the steep fall in the prices of plantation crops, especially that of natural rubber in the international market. It is generally agreed that the crisis in the plantation sector, especially in the case of rubber, has adversely affected the entire rural economy of the state, due to its forward and backward linkages. In Kerala, natural rubber farming occupies second position next to coconut in terms of area with 4,75,039 hectares and provides an average annual employment of more than 30 million mandays. The market price of natural rubber had reached it peak in 1995. From November 1996 onwards, it started declining drastically such that within the next five years the market price of rubber has got almost halved leading to an overall crisis in the rural sector.

Apart from the above transformations in the agricultural sector, there have been two major developments, which bear strong implications on the labour relations in the state. These are the weakening of the trade union movement and the reversal of state patronage.

Labour militancy and restrictive measures of the trade unions came into the limelight of discussions by the 1980s. The 'undemocratic' modes of worker protests such as *bandh* and *gherao* were criticized, not only by the employers and investors but by the common public as well. There has been a strong contention towards the rent seeking and militant behaviour of organised sects of labour, such as head loaders. The closed shop policy, followed by the trade unions led to the development of rentier behaviour within segments of unionised labour that had secured the rights to allocate jobs to its members (Remesh, 2003). Lower levels of productivity and lack of motivation of workers became the image of Kerala's labour, which prompted development thinkers to remark that 'Kerala workers think that non-creation of surplus value is the best way to resist exploitation' (George, 1998). The farm workers agitation during the late 1990s, with crop destruction as its major strategy, also added to the 'militant' image of Kerala worker (Economic and Political Weekly, 1997).

Further to this, in the 1990s the trade unions in the state have been suffering major setbacks, which has in turn led to a massive reduction in their support base among the rural workers. The credibility of trade unions among the workers also eroded considerably, with a continuous decline in their memberships in all the prominent sectors, since the early 1990s. In many a sector the workers were found treating trade unions as a necessary evil or as brokering and rent-seeking institutions between them and the employers. The period witnessed considerable setbacks to trade union movement in the state, with repeated failures in organised collective bargaining and strikes.

A major adversarial outcome of the dishonoured image of Kerala labour was the marked shift in the pro-labour attitude of the governments in the state. Recent decades witnessed a discernible downfall in the domination of trade unions in dictating the government's policies. Since the mid 1980s, the protective policy followed by the state governments towards labour has been exhibiting a drastic reversal, which is characterised by substantial withdrawal of government from welfare measures, dismantling of many social security schemes and decline of workers' co-operative movement. Further, the priorities of government have been shifted towards checking 'pernicious practices' in the labour market and promoting 'investor-friendly' environment[5].

In the backdrop of these developments, of late, there have been some attempts to delineate and expose certain deviations and contrasts with respect to select micro level settings, from the stylized macro features of the labour market. Though these attempts, to some extent, succeeded in discarding the validity of the universal adoption of received conceptualisations, there has been a felt gap in further establishing the message through extensive case studies focusing on specific segments of rural labour markets.

On the whole, there is a growing consensus that the existing theorisations of the state's rural labour market have failed to capture the totality of its dynamics due to the gross neglect of certain underlying transformations such as the emergence of small holding and tree crop based cultivation, crisis in the plantation sector, the waning of the trade union movement and the reversal of pro-labour policies of the state. It is in this context, the present micro empirical study was carried out focusing on the small holding sector of natural rubber plantations. The study attempts to revisit some of the stylized facts that are broadly attributed to the rural labour market of the state such as: (a): strong presence of trade unionism in rural occupations; (b) existence of highly impersonal and institutionalised labour relations with the active involvement of trade unions and government; (c) existence of high rural wage rates with a continued rise in real wages; (d) strong aversion among educated youth towards manual work and (e) active governmental intervention through welfare programmes and protective legislations covering unorganised sector workers in the rural areas.

The selection of rubber tapping in the small holdings for the detailed study was primarily on account of the significance of the sector in terms of employment provision and its peculiarity in terms of work organisation. As discussed earlier, the sector provides more than 30 million man-days of work, annually. Tapping is relatively a new agricultural occupation in rural Kerala which demands specific skill requirements and year round commitment of workers. Further, the atypical work hours and the labour processes involved in tapping also makes the occupation different from that of other rural occupations. In view of the above distinctions a major concern of the study is to understand whether the general conceptualisations and stylized facts of the state's rural labour markets stand valid in the case of tappers in small-scale rubber sector. To provide a background for the analysis of the case study, the subsequent chapter attempts a detailed overview of theoretical and empirical research in understanding the dynamics of rural labour markets.

NOTES

1. Rural labour households are those households, which derive most part of their income during the last 365 days from wages in manual, agricultural and non-agricultural work in the rural areas.
2. This tendency of wages to move together has been empirically tested earlier in the context of the state with respect to the data pertaining to 1964-65 to 1989-90 (Krishnan, 1991). Baby (2003) also establishes similar interrelated movement of wages.
3. Kerala's experience in organising the workers under cooperative umbrella is well documented. For a detailed discussion see Isaac *et al.*, 1998.
4. The welfare fund model of social security for informal sector workers in Kerala is now more than 30 years old. It started with the formation of welfare fund for the toddy tappers in 1969. At present, the state has about 20 welfare funds, which are functional and cover a vast majority of workers in several occupations including workers in small-scale factories, plantations, shops and cooperative institutions; loading and unloading, motor transport, advocate offices, artisanal activities, fishing, handloom weaving, cashew and coir processing.
5. The recent developments such as industrial policy pronouncement, enactment on head load workers and organization of global investment meet and so on are evidences of the changing attitude of government

3

Rural Labour Markets

Theory and Evidence

Analysis of rural labour markets has been an active subject of research in recent decades and various frameworks and approaches have been engaged in the conceptualisation and understanding of the complex relations in varied rural settings. In this chapter, an attempt is made to provide an overview of the major theoretical approaches towards the conceptualisation of rural labour markets and to discuss the limitations in engaging received general theories to explain specific labour market conditions. The chapter also discusses the major empirical research on labour relations in rural areas, with a special focus on the developing country contexts.

Theories of Rural Labour Markets: An Overview

The early conceptualisation of rural labour markets has been mainly through the analysis of wages as a central parameter. Accordingly, the scope of theoretical research was largely confined to explaining the dynamics of wage determination. This was based on the assumption that being the most important parameter in labour contracts, wages reflect to a greater extent, the changes in and the dynamics of rural labour markets (Osmani, 1991). However, despite the proliferation of research and modelling on wages and its determinants, ambiguities still exist while addressing several known features of a typical rural labour market in developing countries such as the coexistence of involuntary unemployment with responsiveness to supply and demand, plasticity of wage rates in some cases coexisting with rigidity in others and so on.

The inability of normal apparatus of supply and demand in explaining the process of wage formation and revision in rural labour markets was widely understood even in the early phases of development economics. The early theorisation of rural wages was concerned primarily with accounting for two stylized facts such as the downward stickness of wages and the existence of wage rates higher than opportunity income of labour, which was often close to zero in densely populated areas with very little opportunities for non farm employment.

Theorisation of wages, are more difficult in the case of less developed rural based economies, like India, which exhibit certain unique characteristics such as absence of general labour market and higher degree of informalisation. Absence of well established labour institutions, simultaneous existence of varieties of wage systems and contracts, close and complex interlinkage of land, labour and credit markets, lower level of moblisation and organisation of workers, preponderence of personal and social ties and so on are some of the major specificities of rural labour markets in India. All these features complicate the theorisation and modelling related to wages and wage formation in the rural set-up. In this context, attention has turned from the contours of supply and demand towards attempts to understand the role of institutions as well as the behaviour of individuals and households in rural societies.

Prominent Theories on Wages

The prominent theories on wages, which formed the basis of explaining labour markets, are: (a) the subsistence wage theory; (b) neo-classical wage theory; and (c) the efficiency wage theory.

The pioneering approach to the wage formation, which dates back to the general and seminal works of classical political economists like Adam Smith, Malthus, Ricardo and Mill,[1] is based on the concept of subsistence level of wages in the long run. Though there are slight variations in their characterisation of secular path of wages, the basic elements are the same (Datt, 1996). Wages were treated as a part of the productive consumption, an essential material necessity of production. In this context a distinction has been drawn between 'natural wage' and `market wage'. The crux of the subsistence theory centres on the argument that there exists a subsistence level of real wages, which supports zero population growth. Wages were seen as physical costs of reproducing labour, in contrast to, as material incentives to induce efforts or disutility of efforts as in the case of later theories (Bhardwaj, 1987). The long run tendency of wages is to conform to this 'natural price' of labour, which usually differs from the market price, fixed in the short run, depending on supply and demand of labour. The underlying idea of all classical theories is that real wages are determined by norms of subsistence, and is explicable in terms of a variety of historical elements along with socio-economic factors. While continuing to hold allegiance to the idea of a given wage, Marx also emphasized the importance of historical elements in wage determination and visualised labour power becoming a 'free' commodity in the dual sense: freed of personal bondage and also freed of means of subsistence and production. The strategies of capitalists in the Marxian analysis are to maximize the difference between the productivity and wages paid out by strengthening the control over the labour process.

The classical approach based on the subsistence wages received severe criticism, on various grounds. The major argument against the subsistence theories is their failure in explaining the substantial regional variation in wages, as evident in the empirical studies. A number of empirical studies suggest evidences against the monotonic straightforward relation suggested between the rate of population growth and real wage rates, as against the postulates of classical theorists. Further, wages are often found more responsive to specific labour market conditions, such as factors related to supply of and demand for labour, rather than to socio-cultural and historical norms (based on a value system), as proposed by the classical economists.

In neo-classical theory, the prices of 'factors of production' along with prices of commodities are determined simultaneously with quantities of outputs, employing the same mechanisms of demand and supply relations for factors and commodities; for which purpose, factor endowments, technological possibilities and consumer preferences are given. The validity of traditional neoclassical theory to give a complete explanation on the wage formation, based on the equilibrium of aggregate demand for and supply of labour was widely questioned even in the context of developed countries. In developing countries, the major drawbacks cited against the neo-classical approach are: (a) the persistence of involuntary unemployment and positive wage rates; (b) the downward rigidity of money wage rates, over prolonged periods; (c) persistence of inefficient (more costly) contracts along with actually existing (or feasible) cheaper contracts; and (d) the existence of near uniform wage rates for a particular type of job, irrespective of the heterogeneity of labour.

While the subsistence wage theories postulated downward wage rigidity, the other important paradigm on wages, popularly known as Efficiency Wage models,[2] attempt to provide explanations for wage rigidity, especially in the downward direction. The basic axiom of the efficiency models lies on the existence of a positive relationship between real wages and labour's effort per unit time (productivity). The theory explains that there is a unique wage level at which the employer's profits are maximised and s/he will not lower the wages beyond that level, because of the fear of a decline in labour productivity, resulting in dwindling profits. It is further assumed that the wage rates generally exceed the opportunity income of labour, which is closed to zero in labour surplus economies of LDCs. Thus, there will be simultaneous existence of involuntary unemployment and higher wages than the market clearing[3].

The earliest version of efficiency wage theories postulates a link between nutrition and efficiency. Assuming such a linkage, a number of nutrition-based efficiency models are constructed. It is primarily this version of efficiency wage theory, which got wider currency in analysing labour markets in developing countries (Jha, 1997). However, like the subsistence theories, efficiency models also fail to explain the empirical realities of regional and temporal variations in wages. Further, the theory clearly contradicts the general reality by postulating that it is the employers, rather than the workers, who resist the wage cut.

Attempts were also made to improvise upon the basic tenets of these theoretical formulations to accommodate the complex empirical realities specific to rural labour market situations. The major among these are the Labour-Turnover Models, Insider-Outsider Models, and Collective Bargaining Models. The Labour-Turnover Models, based on the efficiency wage theories show that under certain circumstances, employers find it profitable to pay wages above the market clearing level (Datt, 1996). This action is, however, not based on a positive effort-wage relation (as postulated in efficiency theory), but on an inverse relation between wages and cost of labour turnover. The crux of the theory is the argument that higher wages reduces turn over costs of labour, either through a reduction in the worker's outflow or by lowering the replacement cost. In the developing country context, Stiglitz (1974) presented the labour-turnover model as an explanation of the gaps between wages and unemployment of rural and urban areas. Further extensions of the model have been attempted by Bardhan (1979), through linking wages and unemployment to variables such as: (i) exogenous increase in labour demand, (ii) recruitment constraining factors; and (iii) supply elasticity of labour. It is widely noted that as the labour turnover models represent a special category within the general class of efficiency wage models they share the same shortcomings.

The Insider-Outsider approach[4], like efficiency wage theories, view that it is the market power in the wage setting that results in the wage rates above the market clearing level. It is suggested that those in employment have some power to disrupt, and hence to share profitability, thereby pushing the wage above the level at which the unemployed would work

(Fine, 1998). The only difference between the insider-outsider theory and that of efficiency wages is the assumption on the market power of agents. In efficiency wage model, the market power rests with the employers, while the insider-outsider model classifies labour into mutually exclusive groups: (1) the insiders who are employed; and (2) the outsiders who are unemployed. The insiders exercise their power to extract a portion of the rent from the employers. As a result, the wage rates are above the market clearing level, which results in unemployment. While discussing the insider-outsider models, Solow (1990) observes that those in unemployment are not necessarily costlessly interchangeable with those in employment. This is because insiders have powers to impose cost on employers, either deliberately through disruption of production or unwittingly as a consequence of hiring costs[5]. The main drawback of this model, like the efficiency wage theory, is its inability to explain the existence of near uniform wage rate for a given task in a given locality in the rural sector.

The collective bargaining models emphasise the importance of organised action of workers in raising the wages. There are several explanations as to how the workers collectivity, generally through trade unionism, interacts with the bargaining structure existing in the specific labour markets. A major subset of the collective bargaining models based on game theoretic exercises, assumes that the transactional outcomes of the labour markets, such as wages and employment, can be characterised in terms of (asymmetric) Nash Bargaining Solutions[6]. Datt (1996) explicates the sum of the approach as follows: *"The key idea is that despite variations in actual bargaining process in village labour markets, their results in terms of the wage and employment outcomes can be approximated by the (asymmetric) Nash bargaining solution. The use of Nash Solution could thus be thought of as 'reduced form' approach to the wage determination problem"*.

Institutional Approaches in Rural Labour Market Analysis

Notwithstanding these theoretical advancements in analysing rural labour markets through wages, many of the empirical realities in rural labour markets remain unexplained. This, in turn, is suggestive of the limitation in the universal application of various theories. Thus, though it is possible to evolve a theory on a high level of abstraction, which is logically consistent and self contained, it may not adequately explain the dynamics of wage formation and labour relations, in all rural labour markets, irrespective of regional, occupational and temporal disparities (Remesh, 2000). The alternative, here, is to evolve an analytical frame based on studies of regional labour markets, across occupations (Papola, 1970). Thus, though there is a place for abstract theory, it cannot legitimately be grounded in the study of labour markets or of a particular labour market without developing the theory in conjunction with the specifics of the labour markets concerned. It is thus argued that the search for a single model and universal application or a 'rule' of wage determination is misplaced, as is the analysis of wage rates in isolation from labour contracts (Omkarnath, 2000). Any labour market theory, thus, must respond and correspond to the specific combinations of socio-economic relations, processes, structures and agents through which the market coordinates the underlying relationship between capital and labour. The widespread understanding of the limitations of general theories has led to development of specific theories on rural labour market giving due recognition to institutional constraints and environments. Thus, of late, the institutional approach based on contractual analysis, has become an important framework in the understanding of the dynamics of the rural labour markets.

The increased prominence of institutional approach in the understanding of agrarian systems is an outcome of the growing concern about the constraints that shapes the rural institutions and about their causes and consequences. According to these theories, contracts allow individuals to make better use of their specific endowments in imperfect markets and to arrive at combinations of income, effort and risk that reflect both their endowments and their states. In environments with heterogeneous labour and market imperfections, different types of contracts do coexist and contractual terms vary across individuals regions and over time.

The central focus of most of the studies within the framework has been the choice between land tenancy and employment contracts. Alternative arrangements or contracts exist in combining labour and means of production in agrarian societies of developing countries. This invokes a 'choice problem' to workers and employers, which is the basic postulate of these models. Modelling efforts within the framework has expanded from the traditional realm of land tenancy to the new frontier of agriculture labour contracts. While the prolific literature on land tenancy has focused on the choice between share and fixed rent tenancy contract (Newberry and Stiglitz, 1979; Binswanger and Rosenswieg, 1984; Quibra and Rashid, 1984; Otsuka and Hayami, 1988; Singh, 1989) studies on agrarian labour relations have mainly focused on the choice between casual and permanent-labour contracts (Bardhan, P.K. 1979, 1983, Eswaran and Kotwal, 1985; Bell and Srinivasan, 1985) or the choice among different remunerative systems for casual labour such as time rates and piece rates.

Though numerous attempts have been made to analyse labour relations in agrarian set-up within the framework of contracts, the outcomes have largely been confined to the formulation of a group of models that shares some general implications. The lack of a well-formulated model is thus a major limitation of the approach. Despite this, the framework is widely engaged as an important tool in understanding the functioning of complex rural labour markets in developing countries (Hayami and Otsuka, 1993).

Rural Labour Markets: A Survey of Empirical Research

In India, studies on labour and working class became prominent only in the first decade after independence. Most of the studies during this period have focused largely on industrial relations taking labour deployment, bargaining practices and conflict behaviour and so on as the objects of systematic investigation (Mohapatra, 1999). Studies on rural labour markets lagged behind, for about two decades. Rural labour markets, as subject of research and analysis, attracted attention only in the seventies and further gathered momentum in the eighties.

Since the early seventies, there have been a number of studies that address the question of rural/agricultural wages, focusing on the trends and pattern of the wages, across time and region using the secondary sources of data (Jose, 1978; Acharya, 1989; Bhalla, 1979; Unni, 1988; Baby, 1996). All these studies came out with substantial evidence on real wage disparities across time, region and occupations, which stand against the postulate of wage fixity at the subsistence level forwarded by the classical theories. Most of these studies, by giving importance to the real wages than nominal wages, stress on the importance of macro economic variables like inflation and cost of living in deciding the actual level of wages, indicated by the effective purchasing power of workers[7]. However, despite the analysis of trends and pattern of wages, these studies do not explain directly the mechanism of wage determination and its revision in the rural setting.

Historical setting of the labour markets is also found important in deciding the wages. The nature of work relationship, the degree of attachment or bondage and the prominence of socio-cultural factors such as caste, evolved over time determine the level of wages, though not directly. Caste and socio-cultural aspects also play a vital role in the wage setting through imposing supply side rigidities. As the traditional rural occupations are caste based, caste acts as a barrier for the inter-occupational mobility of labour, resulting in labour shortage in certain sectors with its abundance in certain others. Caste barriers for entry lead to higher wages in labour-scarce occupations and areas, whereas it depresses wage in labour abundant situations. The village labour markets have evolved over generations, giving enough room to build up personal and social ties. In rural societies, wages are determined often socially without giving much consideration to the economic forces. A bonded labour may receive a bottom level of wages or no-wages, in certain circumstances, as he lacks bargaining power due to the inter-generational ties with the employer. In this context Breman (1993) points out that the per-worker wage will be meagre if all members of a family work with the same employer.

The segmentation of rural labour markets is also documented as an important factor, which affects the functioning of the rural labour markets. It is evident from various studies that the rural labour markets are highly segmented, across regions, occupations, castes and gender (Rao, 1988). All these segmentations affect the wage level in the rural areas, through posing restrictions on the free mobility of labour. Many studies also stress on the importance of locality or village, which demarcates the activity sphere of the workers and employers. It is observed that strict village boundaries are maintained in the operations of factor markets and these limits are often found to be treated as moral boundaries strictly maintained, by both workers and employer (Bardhan, P.K and Rudra, A. 1981; Breman, 1993; Jha, 1997).

Among the other supply side factors, migration assumes some importance. It is observed that higher levels of migration of various categories of workers often lead to depression in wages in the receiving areas[8]. Breman (1993) explains, how the large-scale migration of labour from Maharashtra pulls down the local wages, during the harvest seasons, far below the minimum level of existence, in the rural labour markets of South Gujarat. Studies have also shown that use of women and child labour depresses the general wage level in rural labour markets.

The reserve price of the labour is also found to be important in affecting labour market outcomes. Possession of land holdings, availability of alternative employment opportunities, social security schemes, increase education levels and existence of employment generation programmes are certain factors, which increase the reserve price of labour and thus, necessitate increase in wage levels. Here, comes the role of governmental intervention in determination of wages. It is observed that the cumulative effects of various governmental actions such as: implementation of minimum wages regulations, land reforms social security schemes, employment generation and asset creation programmes and so on favourably influence the level of wages, as it increases the reservation income and hence the bargaining power of labour. The critical role of state in intervening in rural labour processed is found to have significant effect on the formation of rural labour markets. Corroborating this, Omkarnath (1993), observes that the distribution of wastelands and grant of homesteads by the government and the subsidized rice programmes have helped the poor workers to free themselves from labour tying through credit to some extent.

Seasonality of farm operations is often cited as an important factor that decides the level of wages. Studies indicate that landlords are willing to pay a wage higher than the market clearing wages in order to ensure a steady supply of labour in the peak season. This is in line with argument of efficiency theory where a more than market clearing wages is argued to prevail due to the profit maximising behaviour of the employer. At the same time, studies also note that the workers are willing to work for low wages in the peak season, given an assurance that they will get employment in the lean season. While the employers' action of paying higher wages in the lean season shows the importance of seasonality as a factor in deciding wages, the willingness of labour to work below market clearing wages, stress on the influence of employment in deciding wages.

Prevalence of alternative employment opportunities and the existence of higher wages in related sectors are also found pushing up wages. This is especially so in the case of agricultural sector, with the availability of non-farm work which is more attractive, in terms of wages. Bardhan (1973) observes that as non-farm wage employment is a third option for the landless agricultural labour, other than farm work and leasing in of land, given other things, the wage rates for unskilled worker would affect the agricultural wage worker. Krishnan (1991) analysing data related to eight categories of rural workers, for about three decades till 1987, concludes that the wage structure in different occupations maintained the wage differential in the long run. Any increase in the wages of one sector was found leading to proportionate wage increases in the related occupations[9].

The existence of more profitable cash crop sector is found boosting the wages in food crop farming operations. For instance, it is widely recognised that one of the major reasons for a higher level of wages in the paddy sector of Kerala is the existence of a developed cash crop sector. (Unni, 1988; Baby, 1996; Krishnaji, 1991). Similar to this argument, Bardhan, K. (1973) points towards the possibility of higher agricultural wage rates in the industrialised states like Maharashtra and West Bengal, as compared to Orissa.

Among the demand side factors, increase in irrigation facilities and cropping intensity are found positively affecting the wage rates of agricultural labour. This is more so in areas where a smaller proportion of rural labour force are dependent on wage employment and/or with higher non-agricultural wage rates than in areas where vast masses of tiny peasants and the landless flood the labour market and the non-agricultural sector is too small to absorb much of it. This may not happen if the farmers in the former area resort to using a lot of labour saving machinery, or labour in the latter organise themselves for group bargaining.

Another group of researchers looked into the comparative advantage in the bargaining power of labour and employers. It is found that wages are high when workers have higher bargaining capacity, and lower when the employers have more power. A number of modelling attempts (Datt, 1996; Osmani, 1991) analyse the role of collective bargaining in wage determination and has found that the degree of mobilisation and organisation of the workers is a prime factor, which affects the wages and labour relations. It is often highlighted that high level trade unionism among the Kerala labour as the sole determinant of positive wages in the state. Datt (1996) also sees the collective bargaining of the workers (in a tacit way) as the prime factor in wage fixation in agricultural labour markets[10].

On the whole, it can be seen that several factors (economic, social, cultural historical and institutional) were found influencing the wage determination in the rural labour markets. These factors include supply-demand conditions, nature of labour contracts, interlinkage with other factor markets, seasonality, interrelated wage movements and wage relatives, migration, educational status, degree of organisation of labour and so on.

The foregoing discussion suggests that the search for a single model or 'rule' for wage determination and thus, on the formation of rural labour markets is a misplaced effort, considering the diverse and specific settings of regional labour situations. It is equally misleading to analyse wages rates in any rural labour set-up separated or in isolation from other parameters of labour contracts (Omkarnath, 2000). Accordingly a major strand of research treat wages as an integral part of labour and land tenancy contracts and the labour tying mechanisms (Bardhan, P.K. 1979, 1980; Bardhan, K, 1984; Bell and Srinivasan, 1989; Eswaran and Kotwal, 1985; Bardhan, P.K. and Rudra, A. 1981) in analysing rural labour relations, which fall into the framework of New-Institutional theories. The important aspects addressed by these studies are: the existence of multiple contracts; determinants of wage and other contractual parameters; modes and systems of wage payments; the importance of non-wage considerations; and mechanisms of labour tying. This stream of analysis is in line with the prominent school of development thinking in the third world agrarian context (Binswanger and Rosenswieg, 1984; Otsuka and Hayami, 1988; Eswaran and Kotwal, 1985).

Contractual Arrangements in Small Holding Cultivation

In decentralised systems of small holding cultivation, which continues to be a dominant mode of production organisation in agrarian communities world over, various arrangements of land-tenancy and labour-employment contracts are used for combining land and labour. A central concern of small-scale farmers in the selection particular contractual arrangement, from a set of available options, is to minimise costs—both direct as well as indirect related to recruitment, training and monitoring the labour's work-effort to ensure maximum profit. From the workers' point of view, the considerations include minimisation of efforts (in work and for job search), maximisation of returns (wages or product share) and betterment of working conditions, which include leisure, freedom, incentives and flexibilities at work. As some of these objectives are conflicting in nature, the major issue to be resolved is to strike a balance between the antagonistic interests between the contracting parties and to arrive at mutually feasible arrangements.

In small-scale farming arrangements, various labour/employment contracts are used to combine labour and means of production. This availability of options invokes a choice problem to the actors, viz., workers and employers. A major choice is between employment contracts and land contracts (tenancy arrangements). While employment contracts imply engaging of hired workers by the cultivator or landlord, the tenancy arrangements imply transfer of user rights partially or fully to the worker. Here, the landowner receives either a fixed-rent or a stipulated share of the produce. The latter form, though widely prevalent in the agrarian systems of South and Southeast Asian Countries (Bardhan, P.K. and Rudra, A., 1981), is rare to see in small farming systems due to the disincentives posed by the absence of scale economies (Brewster, 1950).

Within the employment contracts, there could be different choices between terms of employment (casual *versus* regular; temporary *versus* permanent), modes of payment (cash wage *versus* product share) and wage payment systems (piece rate wages *versus* time rate wages). An employer may compare the merits as well as disadvantages of different tenures before arriving at his/her decision as to whether to go for a casual/temporary worker or to engage a regular/permanent one. While the engagement of a casual or temporary worker allows the cultivator to get rid of the long-term commitments to the worker (in terms of provision of employment and other wage and non-wage benefits), it also raises a number of disincentives, which include the recurring cost of recruitment of workers, risk of output loss in the absence of committed labour, absence of loyalty from the worker and subsequent loss in terms of productivity, increased monitoring costs and so on. Similarly, a landlord may opt for a long-term or permanent contract if it directly ensures a higher level of long-run prospects of future benefits compared to a casual/temporary employment contract. For instance, several studies suggest a higher likelihood of landlords opting for permanent work arrangements as it enables them to develop strong personal and emotional ties with the labour, which to some extent discourage the latter from shirking and cheating. In agrarian economies, the preference for permanent labour is found to be high if the operations are repetitive/regular and there are constraints for the employer to monitor the enforceability of the contract. On the contrary, employment of casual labour is commonly resorted in short-term farm operations such as weeding and rice transplanting; the result of this work as well as harvesting is relatively easy to measure so that the work of casual labour can be supervised at relatively modest cost even under a time-rate contract or their work incentives can be enhanced by applying a piece rate contract (Roumasset and Uy, 1980).

The approach of the labour towards the contractual tenure would be different. In several instances, short-term contracts provide the workers higher per day wages and freedom from long-term commitments or obligations, compared to long-term contracts. At the same time, these contracts are characterised by the risk of recurring periods of unemployment and job search as well as by lack of patronage from a permanent employer. While permanent contracts enable the landlord to derive loyalty from the labour (which in turn circumvents the former's risk), to the latter it is a means to ensure employment security and extra wage support; and to minimise the efforts of recurring job search. It is often cited in the literature that workers are found preferring long-term contracts with the scope for continuation/renewal, even when the nominal wages are lower[11].

There is ample literature discussing the prevalence of extra-contractual support between the labour and employer in the agrarian societies. Landlords are found supporting their attached labour or tenants in a variety of means such as:

provision of credit, insuring the labour and his/her family in the event of unexpected hazards, giving gifts during festivals and select occasions, extension of assistance during sickness, and using the landlord's connections and influence to solve the tenant's troubles with outside authorities such as police and local administration. The tenant/labour also reciprocates by providing his/her family's loyal service not only in farm production but also in social and political activities of the landowner. It is in this context, various empirical studies (Bardhan, P.K. and Rudra, A. 1981; Bell and Srinivasan, 1989) proposed the theory of 'interlinked markets' postulating that in LDCs, the visible outcomes of the labour markets (such as labour and employment) are highly interlinked to the functioning of related factor markets, such as those of land and credit.

The mutually supporting existence of actors in the agrarian set-up is often explained as a 'patron-client relationship', where a special case of dyadic bondage exists between the interacting parties. This involves a largely instrumental friendship in which an individual of higher economic status (patron) uses his/her own influence and resources to provide protection and/or benefits for a person of lower status (client), who in turn, reciprocates by offering general support and assistance, including personal services to the patron (Scott, 1976). In such a relationship, transactions are multi-stranded and the balance clearing is schemed in the long run. The multiple transactions between the two parties, spanning into several years and across goods and services, as manifested in the patron client-relationship, is often viewed as a device to reduce transaction costs because much of the cost of collecting information and contractual enforcement is common to all transactions (Bardhan, P.K. 1980; Kikuchi and Hayami, 1980; Hayami and Otsuka, 1993).

Interlinking of markets also work as an effective device in enforcing the contractual terms in agrarian communities (Binswanger and Rosenswieg, 1984; Hayami and Otsuka, 1993; Narayana and Nair, 1989). As small agrarian communities in developing countries are typically characterised by close personal relationships between landlord and tenant the contractual arrangements are more or less unwritten or oral, where details are often implicit than spelt out. The enforcement of such contracts is often enabled through nurturing of personal and social ties. As Hayami and Otsuka (1993) observes: *"In small agrarian communities social interactions among people are intense. Everyone is watching everyone. One party's dishonest behaviour tends to be detected by neighbours in the community and conveyed to another party by word of mouth. In such a community, both parties may be discouraged from behaving dishonestly given the severe cost of loss of reputation in the event of discovery"*.

Another major aspect of contractual choice in agrarian societies is the mode of payment (cash wage *versus* product share). From the viewpoint of the employer, cash wage payment system may be more beneficial if the prevailing product prices are fairly high. In contrast to this, the preference for remunerating labour with share of the produce would be more, in times of dwindling product markets and when there are uncertainties and risks attached to the market price of the produce. For instance, a farmer may prefer to pay the worker in terms of agricultural produce, if there are no adequate warehousing facilities and if there is a considerable lag between the harvest and sale of product. Conversely, the preference of worker regarding mode of payment would be more inclined towards cash payments than product share, if the produce fetches lower price in the market and *vice versa*. Thus, both the actors are found to be interested in choosing such an arrangement that circumvents risks and maximizes expected returns.

Yet another concern in the choice of agrarian contracts is the system of wage payment (piece rate *versus* time rate). Here also, the employers' preference for a particular system would vary according to his/her perception regarding the pay-offs. It is more likely that a farmer would prefer to employ his/her worker(s) in a time-rate wage system, if the contract is easily enforceable; the effort is less costly to monitor; and its output, tangible or separable. For instance, in casual and short-term operations, the employer may find time rate payment feasible, as it is relatively easy and less costlier to supervise the effort of the worker. However, the preference would tilt in favour of piece rate, if the work-efforts were costlier to monitor. A piece rate system along with a stipulation for quality check allows the employer to free himself/herself from the hassles of supervision and monitoring. Thus, transaction cost minimisation becomes a prime consideration in the selection of wage payment system for the employer. If the employer is concerned with enforcement cost, the workers are more interested in incentives. A piece rate system provides more incentive to a worker than the time rate system, especially when the worker is industrious.

As the preferences of contracting parties are bound to vary due to their conflicting objective functions, it is often the power relations between the actors that matter while resolving the choice problems in contractual selection. The factors that add to the comparative advantage of the small farmers include the degree of collectivity among themselves; the scope and resource availability for supervision and monitoring; the nature of the crop (which delimits the farmers' scope for controlling product loss); the facilities available for warehousing and for effective marketing of the produce; higher product prices and close access to product markets. On the other hand, for the labour, their comparative bargaining power would be directly linked to the degree of collectivity and individual reservation prices.

In a small holder farming situation where the farmers are more organised than the workers, it is bound to see that the former enjoys more freedom and power in deciding contractual forms and deciding terms of contractual arrangements. Conversely, in a situation where the small holders are either less organised or unorganised compared to the rural labour households, the latter can considerably influence the supply decisions in the labour market. But the small holders, as they are less organised, are not able to influence decisions regarding labour demand. Unlike their counterparts in the interlinked markets, the stake of the small holders is very weak and they tend to be at the receiving end in contractual situations (Nair, 1997).

The reservation prices of the workers in rural labour markets are closely linked to the opportunity costs (available alternative employment) and the resource endowment of the worker. In a small holder agricultural situation, if the workers are backed with some income generating assets such as land or property, it obviously tilts the nature of labour tying mechanisms or contractual arrangements to their favour. For instance, there is a wider consensus among the researchers that redistributive measures such as land reforms would lead to the restructuring of contractual arrangements that give more leverage to the erstwhile landless labour. From the above discussion, it is clear that in small-scale farming arrangements, various labour-employment contracts exist, which are shaped by a number of factors.

Understanding the emergence of contractual arrangements, the choice of particular contract systems, the enforcement of contractual terms and adaptability of institutions in response to economic forces, changes in the structural parameters and the policy environment could provide valuable insights into the functioning of rural labour markets. In this backdrop, the detailed case study of tappers attempted in the dissertation underlines the binding parameters of labour tying arrangements, which determine the dynamics of rural labour relations. The subsequent chapter provides the profile of rubber cultivation in Kerala, the details of the study area; the process involved in tapping and discusses the analytical tool as well as the hypotheses under examination.

NOTES

1. For a detailed account on classical wage theory, see Stirati, A. (1994).
2. The original contributions of this theory can be seen in Leibenstien, 1957. The model has been later elaborated by Mirlees, 1975; Rodgers, 1975; Stiglitz, 1976. For a extensive exposition on efficiency models see Stiglitz, 1976; Akerlof 1984; Yellen, 1984; Akerlof and Yellen, 1986.
3. Akerlof (1984) puts this as follows: "If there is involuntary unemployment in equilibrium situation, it must be that firms, for some reason or other, wish to pay more than the market clearing wage. And that is the heart of efficiency wage theory".
4. For a detailed exposition of Insider-Outsider models, see Lindbeck and Dennis (1988); and Blanchflower *et al.* (1990).

5. The insider-outsider explanation could also be related to the concepts of 'rent seeking' and solidarity within the firm. Solow (1990) argues that insiders are in a position to bargain with the firm over the division of the rent. The rent may arise simply because the insiders are more productive in this firm than outsiders would be. It will be enlarged if the insiders can jointly threaten to resist the hiring of outsiders by refusing them to train them or to cooperate with them. That may require a certain amount of solidarity.
6. The implicit cooperative theory or the tacit-collective bargaining model presented by Osmani (1991) is a typical example for the game theoretic approach to explain collective bargaining in the rural labour markets. Using the framework of non-cooperative repetitive game, the process of wage determination of daily wage earners is viewed as an act of implicit cooperation. This in turn explains the co-existence of involuntary unemployment and wage rigidity in the downward direction. Krishnan (1991) also corroborates this, in explaining the social stigma that prevents the rural labour in Kerala to undercut wages.
7. Though the deflating of the nominal wages with index of consumer price, as attempted in these studies, is found reasonable, there are still doubts related to the use of general consumer price index for all the regions within the states, taking into consideration the intrastate differences in the actual cost of living. For instance, Baby (1996) argues that it is better to use certain proxies, like district-wise price of paddy, for deflating the nominal wages of agricultural labour across various districts.
8. An increase in the wages in the 'donor' areas due to out-migration is generally not valid in the LDCs, which are characterised by the presence of excess labour who are either involuntarily unemployed or underemployed.
9. In Kerala, the increase in the wages of construction workers during the seventies due to the 'construction boom' has led to a proportionate increase in the wages of all related occupations, thus keeping the social hierarchy of occupations intact (Krishnan, 1991).
10. The model is similar to the implicit cooperative theory proposed by Osmani (1991)
11. While discussing the labour tying mechanisms in rural West Bengal, Bardhan, P.K. and Rudra, A. (1981) highlight the extra-wage support given by the employer as an important factor that decides the level of wages. It is explained that the labourers may opt for a low level wages, if there is a scope for other benefits from the employer over and above the contractual obligations.

4

Labour Relations in Rubber Cultivation

Towards a Framework

India is the third largest producer of natural rubber in the world after Thailand, Indonesia and Malaysia and is at the same time the fourth largest consumer after USA, Japan and South Korea (Government of Kerala, 2003). Rubber cultivation in India had been traditionally confined to the narrow belt extending from Kanyakumari district of Tamil Nadu to Dakshin Kannada and Kodagu districts of Karnataka state in the north, and lying in general west of the Western Ghats and parallel to them for approximately 400 km. (Rubber Board, 2000). Within this zone, the state of Kerala assumes considerable significance, with 84 per cent of the area and about 92 per cent of rubber production (Government of Kerala, 2003).

In this chapter, a broad profile of rubber cultivation in Kerala is discussed indicating its significance in the state's economy. A brief account of the structural transformations in rubber cultivation and the labour process involved in tapping of rubber, which is regular and significant category of work involved in rubber cultivation is also provided. Further, the chapter provides an account of the profile of study regions, data and methodology of the survey and outlines the hypotheses examined in the subsequent analysis. The analytical tool of principal agent relationship is also discussed in this chapter.

Prominence of Natural Rubber in Kerala's Economy

Natural rubber plays a vital role in the agrarian economy of the state as the share of the crop in the total cropped area is 15.7 per cent, contributing 15.2 per cent of the state's agricultural gross domestic product (Lekshmi and George, 2003). Rubber cultivation in the state is said to have begun in the early 20th century and within the span of 100 years[1], the crop has expanded tremendously taking the total area of cultivation to roughly 4,75,000 hectares. The progress in the expansion of area was more pronounced during the 1950s and 1960s. This was partly due to the fact that rubber cultivation was almost confined to Kerala and during these years agrarian reforms in the state were only in the anvil. Since the legislation had proposed to exempt rubber and the other plantation crops from the purview of land ceiling, a considerable extent of area under coconut and arecanut was brought under rubber. Further, widespread prevalence of root wilt disease of coconut in the Central Kerala and a relatively remunerative price for rubber during the period fuelled the process of crop-shift in favour of rubber. However, owing to a prolonged sluggishness in the rubber market, the period 1970 to 1977 suffered a major setback in the process of expansion of area.

The average annual rate of new planting, which was 12,000 ha. during the period 1956 to 1962 and 6,000 ha. during 1963 to 1970 came down to 4,200 ha. By the late 1970s, the situation, however, changed and there was in fact a boom in new planting activity. This could be ascribed to the upward trend in the price of rubber, coupled with incentives introduced by the Rubber Board in the form of cash subsidy for new planting.

The average annual rate of new planting during the first half of the 1980s was around 20,000 ha. and the total area under rubber increased to nearly 2,83,000 ha. by 1985-86. Though there were short-term fluctuations, the pace of area expansion continued and by 1998-99, the total area under the crop reached 55,400 ha. with 3,87,000 ha. under tapping. The lower labour absorption capacity of the crop (against crops like paddy) is also considered to have influenced the spread of the crop. Of late, there is a widespread contention that the higher wages and militant labour situation in Kerala during the past few decades tempted more and more farmers to shift the cropping pattern in the state, in favour of rubber. The acute shortage in irrigation (due to the remarkable increase in total cropped area in the state), in recent decades, is argued to have further forced farmers to shift towards less water demanding crops like rubber. This is specially true with the tail-end farmers of large-scale surface irrigation projects, who found transacting irrigation water extremely costly, which prompted a shift towards cost minimising crops (Neetha, 2003). All these explanations point towards the centrality of comparative profitability of rubber in guiding the shift in cropping pattern in the state, in favour of natural rubber. Table 4.1. gives details

Table 4.1: Total Area, Tapped Area, Production and Average Yield Per Hectare of Rubber in Kerala

Year	Total area (ha.)	Tapped area (ha.)	Production (Tonnes)	Average yield per hectare (kg)*
1955-56	80537 (93.6)	62399 (92.9)	21680 (91.4)	347 (-6)
1960-61	135809 (94.4)	65355 (93.0)	23175 (90.2)	354 (-11)
1965-66	174561 (93.5)	106623 (94.6)	46953 (92.9)	440 (-8)
1970-71	198424 (91.4)	134103 (95.0)	86773 (94.1)	647 (-6)
1975-76	211808 (89.8)	167742 (94.0)	128769 (93.5)	768 (-4)
1980-81	253784 (89.3)	179980 (92.7)	140320 (91.7)	780 (-8)
1985-86	341506 (89.2)	205780 (92.1)	184563 (92.1)	897 (-1)
1990-91	407821 (85.8)	284960 (93.0)	307521 (93.3)	1079 (3)
1991-92	419174 (85.8)	301360 (92.9)	343109 (93.6)	1139 (9)
1992-93	428864 (85.9)	306539 (92.8)	368648 (93.7)	1203 (12)
1993-94	437138 (86.0)	313416 (92.6)	408311 (93.8)	1304 (19)
1994-95	443300 (86.0)	318965 (92.1)	442830 (93.9)	1389 (27)
1995-96	449000 (85.7)	328812 (92.3)	474555 (93.6)	1443 (21)
1996-97	455566 (85.4)	335400 (91.7)	512756 (93.3)	1529 (26)
1997-98	465282 (85.5)	342420 (90.8)	541935 (92.8)	1583 (34)
1998-99	469924 (85.0)	349683 (90.3)	559099 (92.4)	1590 (36)
1999-00	472900 (84.7)	355342 (90.0)	572820 (92.1)	1612 (36)
2000-01	474364 (84.3)	359780 (90.0)	579866 (92.0)	1612 (36)
2001-02	475039 (83.9)	360006 (89.8)	580350 (91.9)	1612 (36)

Source: Rubber Board (2000): Indian Rubber Statistics, Vol. 24.

Note: (1) Figures in parentheses except the last column give share of Kerala in the total estimates of the country.
(2) *Figures in parentheses give difference from all India estimates.
(3) Because of low rubber prices, productivity was stagnant during 1999-2000 to 2001-02.

of rubber cultivation in India and Kerala, in terms of production, area under cultivation and yield of the crop.

From the table, it is evident that in terms of area under cultivation and production, Kerala accounts for bulk of the country's rubber production with 90.3 per cent of tapped area and 92 per cent of total production respectively. The higher productivity (yield per acre) figures of Kerala indicate the increased profitability of rubber cultivation in the state than elsewhere in the country[2].

Pattern of Rubber Plantations in Kerala

Dominance of Small and Tiny Holdings

A salient feature of the rubber plantation industry in the country is the dominance enjoyed by the small holding sector, as a result of a major structural change. In its early phases, like other plantation crops, rubber also was prominently raised in estates and larger haciendas[3]. However, gradually, medium and small holdings emerged in the scene in a prominent way as more and more area were brought under rubber, as a reflection to the highly remunerative prices existed in the industry. Following the categorisation of Rubber Board, the rubber plantations could be broadly divided into two: (a) estate sector, representing big haciendas; and (b) holding sector, comprising of medium, small and tiny holdings. The cut of point of these two categories is 20 hectares (50 acres).

In 1925, holdings of 40 hectares (100 acres) and below in size occupied 27 per cent of the total area under rubber. During the period 1925 to 1928, the increase in the area of small holdings was at a greater pace than estates. As a result, the share of holdings in the total area increased to 41 per cent in 1928. (Government of India, 1968) However, the visible depression in the agricultural sector marked with a slump in the price of agricultural commodities in general and that of rubber in particular affected the expansion in rubber cultivation. In 1932, the rubber prices touched an unprecedented lower level. Further to this, in 1934, the

International Rubber Regulation Act (IIRA) came, whereby production and new planting of rubber was restricted. All these constrained the expansion of the crop, whereby the small holdings lost their initial tempo of expansion. Between 1936 and 1942, the area under small holdings of 100 acres (40 hectares) and below in size was only 5,839 acres (2,363 hectares) as compared with 13,671 acres (5,533 hectares) of estates.

However, the onset of II World War changed the situation. By 1942 as most of the rubber producing regions in South East Asia was occupied by Japan, 90 per cent of world's sources of natural rubber was cut off to the Allied Nations[4]. As a result of this, the growers of India and Ceylon were encouraged to produce more rubber by exploiting the trees to the maximum. IIRA was removed in 1942 and there were considerable activities in rubber planting and replanting. The immediate period subsequent to war was not a good state for the industry as the trees had been exploited to the maximum. Low-level yield, coupled with unimpressive price for rubber, forced the small growers to abandon rubber cultivation or to switch over to other remunerative crops (such as tapioca and pepper), which resulted in progressive decline of planting in small holding sector.

During 1951-52, the total output of rubber increased to 18,000 tonnes (as against the average of 16,000 tonnes in 1940-50), out of which 28 per cent was contributed by small holdings of 40 hectares (100 acres) and below size. The estate sector shared as much as 55 per cent of the area during 1955-56. When the Plantation Labour Act was promulgated in 1951, many growers were forced to limit the size of their holding within 10 ha. These as well as division of property under the prevailing land ownership systems resulted in fragmentation of units. Further, on account of relatively remunerative price of rubber, a large segment of small and marginal land holding shifted their cropping pattern in favour of rubber. Consequently, during 1957-58, the share of area under the small holding sector surpassed that of estates. The price slump of tea during 1970 led many small-scale tea growers to shift to rubber cultivation. The small holding (below 20 ha.) sector, which accounted for 33.2 per cent of the rubber area in India in 1947 sharply moved to 86.1 per cent by 1996-97. About 86 per cent of the area and production of rubber is contributed by the small holding sector, which is composed of 9,58,000 units (Rubber Board, 1998). From 1947 to 1996-97, the number of tiny holdings (below 2 ha.) in the small holding sector had increased 68 times, the relative increase in area being 49 times. Notably, the average size of a rubber small holding in the country is less than one hectare. However, as said elsewhere the categorisation of Rubber Board considers all holdings under 20 hectares (50 acres) as small holdings, while holdings above the cut off point comes under estates. A disaggregation of holding and estates based on this categorisation is provided in Table 4.2.

The dominance of holding sector over estate sector in rubber cultivation is evident from the table with holding sector accounting for about 88 per cent of the total area under rubber. As has been seen, Kerala accounts for the largest share of rubber cultivation and hence the national picture reflects the trend in the state as well. However, in Kerala the holding sector accounts for about 91 per cent of the total area, which is 3 per cent higher than the national average. More significantly, the share of holding sector has shown a gradual increase over the period as is given in Figure 4.1.

Apart from the domination of holdings in rubber cultivation, there exists concentration of holdings in particular land size class. Within the holding sector, holdings below 4 hectares dominated with about 93 per cent of the area (Table 4.3). A recent study reports that the share of small holdings with an average size of less than 2 hectares in total area under rubber has increased from 53 per cent in 1955-56 to more than 83 per cent in 2001, where the average holding size has declined to less than 0.5 ha. (Viswanathan *et al.*, 2003). Though there is no disaggregate data available for Kerala across size of holdings, there is a consensus that the above pattern is more or less applicable to Kerala, as the state account for the lion share of the area under the crop. On the whole, it could be concluded that within a span of about a century since its advent, the crop has expanded in the state with a clear bias towards the holding sector, especially tiny and small holdings.

Table 4.2: Area of Rubber under Holdings and Estates (In Hectares)

Year	*Kerala*			*India*		
	Holdings	*Estates*	*Total*	*Holdings*	*Estates*	*Total*
1960-61	88366	47443	135809	90375	53530	143905
	(65.1)	(34.9)	(100.0)	(62.8)	(37.2)	(100.0)
1965-66	118675	55886	174561	123010	63703	186713
	(68.0)	(32.0)	(100.0)	(65.9)	(34.1)	(100.0)
1970-71	142611	55813	198424	149800	67398	217198
	(71.9)	(28.1)	(100.0)	(69.0)	(31.0)	(100.0)
1975-76	159805	52003	211808	168687	67189	235876
	(75.5)	(24.6)	(100.0)	(71.5)	(28.5)	(100.0)
1980-81	206056	47728	253784	215443	68723	284166
	(81.2)	(18.8)	(100.0)	(75.8)	(24.2)	(100.0)
1985-86	293847	47659	341506	310209	72622	382831
	(86.0)	(14.0)	(100.0)	(81.0)	(19.0)	(100.0)
1990-91	362240	45581	407821	397465	77618	475083
	(88.8)	(11.2)	(100.0)	(83.7)	(16.3)	(100.0)
1995-96	406642	42358	449000	449499	74576	524075
	(90.6)	(9.4)	(100.0)	(85.8)	(14.2)	(100.0)
1996-97	413274	42292	455566	459437	73809	533246
	(90.7)	(9.3)	(100.0)	(86.2)	(13.8)	(100.0)
1997-98	423215	42067	465282	474880	69654	544534
	(91.0)	(9.0)	(100.0)	(87.2)	(12.8)	(100.0)
1998-99	428002	41922	469924	483701	69340	553041
	(91.1)	(8.9)	(100.0)	(87.5)	(12.5)	(100.0)
1999-00	431213	41687	472900	490277	68307	558584
	(91.2)	(8.8)	(100.0)	(87.8)	(12.2)	(100.0)
2000-01	433559	40806	474365	495358	67312	562670
	(91.4)	(8.6)	(100.0)	(88.0)	(12.0)	(100.0)
2001-02	434457	40582	475039	498961	67594	566555
	(91.5)	(8.5)	(100.0)	(88.1)	(11.9)	(100.0)

Source: Rubber Board (2003): *Indian Rubber Statistics*, Vol. 26.
Note: Figures in parentheses are percentages to respective totals.

The major reasons for the unprecedented expansion of rubber in the small holding sector could be attributed to:

(*a*) *Profitability*: There was a phenomenal increase in the productivity and price of rubber since 1950s leading to higher profitability. The relative profitability of rubber has also remained attractive *vis-à-vis* other crops such as coconut, arecanut, tea, plantain, tapioca and so on.

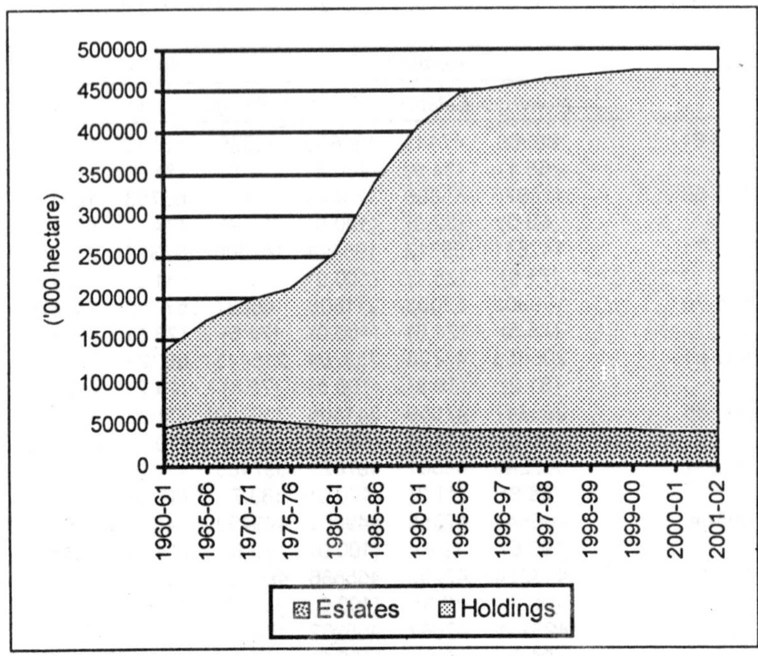

Source: Rubber Board (2003): *Indian Rubber Statistics*, Vol. 24.

Fig. 4.1: Area of Rubber under Holdings and Estates, Kerala, 1960/61-1999/2000

(b) *Smaller Gestation Period and Regular Flow of Income*: One of the reasons for the increased adoption of rubber in the small holdings is its smaller gestation period (5-8 years) compared to traditional varieties of coconut (12-15 years), which is the prominent alternative tree crop. Apart from this, rubber assures a more or less regular flow of income, which is evenly spread over the year.

(c) *Institutional Interventions:* The extension services and subsidies introduced by the Rubber Board and the exemption of crop from the ceiling limit of the Agrarian Relations Act are the major institutional interventions that prompted a high rate of adoption of the crop. The major promotional measures followed by the Rubber

Board include free or subsidized distribution of saplings and other inputs, training in cultivation and farm management practices, launching of targeted promotional programmes such as *Rubber to the Poor,* provision of market information and organisation of small growers societies.

Table 4.3: Distribution of Area under Rubber according to Holdings Size: India

(Area in hectares)

Year	*Upto 2 ha.*	*2-4 ha.*	*Above 4 ha.*	*Total*
1955-56	20489 (53.2)	5699 (14.8)	12300 (32.0)	38488 (100.0)
1960-61	52340 (57.9)	13981 (15.5)	24054 (26.6)	90375 (100.0)
1965-66	72433 (58.9)	18051 (14.7)	32526 (26.4)	123010 (100.0)
1970-71	82570 (55.1)	25853 (17.3)	41377 (27.6)	149800 (100.0)
1975-76	92386 (54.8)	29235 (17.3)	47066 (27.9)	168687 (100.0)
1980-81	139809 (64.9)	30140 (14.0)	45494 (21.1)	215443 (100.0)
1985-86	238158 (76.8)	28071 (9.1)	43980 (14.2)	310209 (100.0)
1990-91	332401 (83.6)	33149 (8.3)	31915 (8.0)	397465 (100.0)
1991-92	342010 (83.3)	35569 (8.7)	33044 (8.1)	410623 (100.0)
1992-93	351571 (83.5)	36450 (8.7)	33138 (7.9)	421159 (100.0)
1993-94	359451 (83.6)	37205 (8.7)	33437 (7.8)	430093 (100.0)
1994-95	365654 (83.6)	37849 (8.7)	34016 (7.8)	437519 (100.0)
1995-96	375957 (83.6)	39079 (8.7)	34463 (7.7)	449499 (100.0)
1996-97	384008 (83.6)	40145 (8.7)	35284 (7.7)	459437 (100.0)
1997-98	394412 (83.1)	44104 (9.3)	36364 (7.7)	474880 (100.0)
1998-99	402326 (83.1)	44515 (9.2)	36850 (7.6)	483701 (100.0)
1999-00	407601 (83.1)	45031 (9.2)	37645 (7.7)	490277 (100.0)
2000-01	412574 (83.3)	45088 (9.1)	37696 (7.6)	495358 (100.0)
2001-02	414146 (83.0)	45803 (9.2)	39012 (7.8)	498961 (100.0)

Source: Rubber Board (2000): *Indian Rubber Statistics*, Vol. 24
Note: Figures in parentheses are percentages to respective totals.

Spatial Variations in the Expansion of Crop in Kerala

The crop was initially dominant only in the Travancore-Cochin Region of the state and it spread to other regions, especially to North Kerala with the migration of farmers from southern and central Kerala, towards Northern districts, in search of cheap and fertile lands. The Table 4.4 shows the regional spread of the crop, after about a century since its advent.

Table 4.4: District-wise Area under Rubber, 1998-99

(In hectares)

Districts	*Nature of Operation*		
	Holdings	*Estates*	*Total*
Thiruvananthapuram	26585 (96.8)	887 (3.2)	27472 (100.0)
Kollam	27026 (74.5)	9249 (25.5)	36275 (100.0)
Alappuzha	3722 (100.0)	-	3722 (100.0)
Pathanamthitta	41421 (87.1)	6149 (12.9)	47570 (100.0)
Kottayam	106182 (96.1)	4366 (3.95)	110548 (100.0)
Idukki	33752 (88.8)	4260 (11.2)	38012 (100.0)
Ernakulam	53340 (94.8)	2903 (5.2)	56243 (100.0)
Thrissur	8982 (67.6)	4308 (32.4)	13290 (100.0)
Palghat	27459 (96.2)	1091 (3.8)	28550 (100.0)
Malappuram	25751 (90.2)	2793 (9.8)	28544 (100.0)
Kozhikode	13938 (78.1)	3906 (21.9)	17844 (100.0)
Wynad	6279 (99.1)	58 (0.9)	6337 (100.0)
Kasargod	21264 (96.8)	699 (03.2)	21963 (100.0)

Source: Rubber Board (2000): *Indian Rubber Statistics*, Vol. 24.
Note: Figures in parentheses are percentages to respective totals.

From Table 4.4 it is evident that Travancore-Cochin Region constitutes the dominant belt of rubber cultivation in the state. Within the region, the three districts of Kottayam, Ernakulam and Pattanamthitta together hold for about 50 per cent of the area in the state. Malabar region still lags behind with only about 26 per cent.

On the whole, it could be summed up that natural rubber cultivation in Kerala has undergone a visible structural transformation, through which the small holding sector has emerged as the prominent segment. The process of decentralisation in farming, caused by sub-division and fragmentation of rubber farms, has gained further momentum with the launching of targeted programmes such as *Rubber to the Poor,* with local level participation[5] (Kurien, 2001). This structural devolution have been uniquely compared to other plantation crops and has given rise to various agro-management issues with serious implications in the labour market (Viswanathan *et al.*, 2003). Though no authentic estimate is available on the number of workers engaged in holding sector and estates, it is beyond argument that rubber holdings assume a major role in employment provision in rural areas, despite their comparatively low labour absorption capacity.

Labour Use and Employment in Rubber Plantations

In India, around three-fourth of the development cost of rubber plantations and 60 per cent of the mature phase costs are accounted for by labour alone. The structural transformation of the rubber plantations during the last five decades, characterised by the disintegration of the estate sector and dominance of the small holdings, had profound impact on the pattern of labour utilisation, organisation and management. Rubber provides direct employment to over 0.34 million people in India (Table 4.5). Though separate data on employment in rubber sector for the state is not available, it is estimated that more than 95 per cent of total employment in the country is accounted by the state alone. Thus, it is accepted that the All India employment figures could be considered as more or less same for the state. The current estimated labour intensity in rubber plantations is 0.62 per ha. The progress of employment

Table 4.5: Average Daily Employment in Rubber Plantations: India

Year	*Numbers*	*Percentage difference between periods*
1965	122481	—
1970	146591	16.4
1975	157754	7.1
1980	192578	18.1
1985	227780	15.5
1990	282674	19.4
1991	293108	3.6
1992	304618	3.8
1993	310800	2.0
1994	315900	1.6
1995	322300	2.0
1996	328900	2.0
1997	335450	2.0
1998	341320	1.7
1999	345000	1.1

Source: Rubber Board (2000).

generation in this sector since 1961, given in Table 4.5 shows that over a span of 35 years the employment generation in the rubber plantation sector has registered a threefold increase. Around 60 per cent of the labour is estimated to be tappers while the rest are general field workers. Apart from this, other related activities such as processing, transportation and marketing of rubber provide considerable employment avenues.

Accordingly, the labour requirement in rubber holdings broadly could be categorized into three stages such as planting, immature phase and mature phase. Whatever may be the stage, labour is required annually or seasonally for application of manures and fertilizers and weeding. The labour requirement during the planting stage are mainly on account of clearing of land; terracing, lining, pitting, filling of pits, budding/nursery management, and field planting/vacancy filling. The major heads of labour requirement in the immature phase are vacancy filling, mulching of plant bases, cover crop establishment and maintenance, shading and propping, branch introduction, thinning out of weak trees. In the mature phase labour is mainly required for tapping and processing. Other labour requirements during this stage are for panel protection, application of stimulants and rain guarding. The labour requirement in this stage is also highly affected by seasonality. Tapping is a year round activity, with some off days during rainy season and during the period of tapping rest (4-6 weeks)[6]. During the rainy months of June-August tapping operation is almost suspended. However, during this season some tapping becomes possible during short intervals of rain free days, if the trees are rain guarded. Estimates suggests that rain guarding could enhance the quantum of employment by 40-45 days (Pothen *et al.*, 2000).

The small growers depend mainly on family labour for many operations. Among the small holding 29 per cent of the labour requirement during the immature phase is met with family labour and the share of female is 14 per cent. In the small holdings, since the tapper himself processes the latex or carries the material to the collection centre or processing units, no separate labour for processing exist. Crude estimates suggest that the small holding sector generates an average annual employment of 38.7 million mandays. The average annual labour requirement in the small holding sector is estimated to be 160-180 days per ha (Burger *et al.*, 1995, Pothen *et al.*, 2000)[7]. In small holdings the tapper requirement per unit area is found to be higher compared to that of estates due to higher tapping intensity (Rubber Board, 2000). These estimates *inter alia* highlight the significance of small holdings in employment provision, despite the comparatively lower labour absorption capacity of the crop[8].

Processes and Systems in Tapping

Tapping is the most labour absorbing and regular operation in rubber holdings, during the mature phase[9]. It is a highly skilled activity, which includes, apart from cutting the bark, a number of related activities such as removal of coagula, collection and transportation of latex and coagula, and sheet preparation. Tapping operation has to be commenced as early as possible in each morning, because the tree bleed less in the hottest part of the day. The tapper makes a spiral cut in the bark of the tree (after removing the coagula), sets a container at its base and then moves to the next tree, few meters away. Usually a tapper attends about 300-400 trees in a morning[10]. After this, following a break of about one hour (which is generally devoted for having breakfast and leisure), the collection of yield begins, with the tapper going back to the first tree and carrying the latex to a central point, where the rubber sheet is prepared in a tray, through a chemical treatment. Afterwards the water from the sheet would be squeezed by slowly and uniformly pressing it with the help of a roller. The sheets would be then dried (either by hanging it in the sunlight or keeping it in smoke houses[11]). The colour, dryness and cleanliness are the important quality parameters for rubber sheets.

Tapping is a year round activity, with some off days during rainy season[12] and the period of tapping rest[13]. Number of trees available to a worker for a day's work is known as tapping task. In an operational sense, a block of trees (300-400)[14] is considered as the adequate tapping task to fully engage a worker. The employment in holdings is a function of tapping task and the system of tapping. In terms of frequency of tapping, the major patterns of tapping in the small holdings could be divided into three: D/1, D/2 and D/3. D/1 refers to continuous daily tapping without any off day in between; D/2 stands for tapping on alternative days and D/3, for tapping on every third day. A holding with 300-400 trees and D/1 tapping pattern can provide employment to a worker throughout the year/season. The same level of employment could be derived from a holding with 600-800 trees in D/2 pattern of tapping or 900-1200 trees in D/3 pattern. The higher the interval between the tapping days, the better would be the yield. Accordingly agencies such as Rubber Board recommends for the observance of D/2 or D/3 pattern of tapping. While the above systems denote the patterns of regular tapping, *slaughter tapping*[15] is resorted in holdings, where the trees have completed their productive life length (i.e., after about 20-25 years of tapping).

Data, Profile of Study Areas and Methodology

As elaborated in Chapter I, the major objectives of the field study include the exploration of issues related to employment, wages and contractual arrangements/labour tying mechanisms; analysis of changing employment relations; and the examination of livelihood diversification process of tappers and tapper households in the small holding sector.

The field data for the study was mainly generated as a part of a national level, multi-centric research project on *Contractual Arrangements in Plantation Sector* conducted by the author at the V.V. Giri National Labour Institute, NOIDA[16]. The survey was carried out in the three Districts of Kottayam, Ernakulam and Thiruvananthapuram in the Travancore-Cochin Region, the prominent belt of small holding rubber cultivation in Kerala. These districts were selected on the basis of their visible prominence in terms of total area under rubber cultivation and the proportion of small holdings in the total

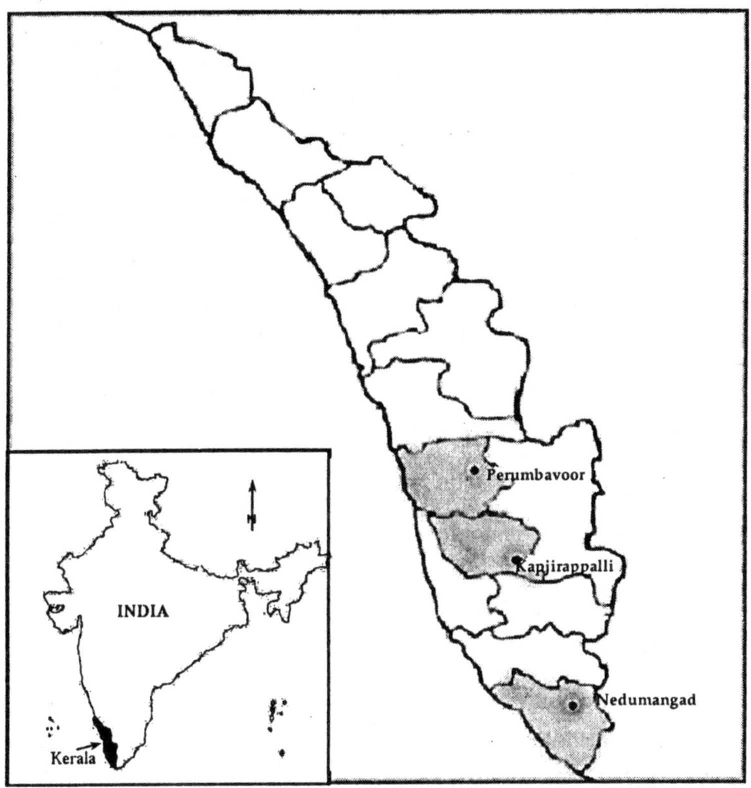

Fig. 4.2: Location of Study Areas

area under rubber (Table 4.4). From these districts, three Taluks (Kanjirappally in Kottayam; Nedumangad in Thiruvananthapuram and Perumbavoor in Ernakulam) were selected purposively, (Figure 4.2), considering two norms such as: vintage of the gardens and average size of holdings. Kanjirappally has a long history of rubber plantation (nearly 100 years) and is characterised with comparatively larger small holdings. Nedumangad and Perumbavoor assume second and third positions respectively, in terms of plantation history (40-60 years and 20-40 years respectively) and size of holdings. From each of these Taluks, three panchayats were selected considering the density of rubber holdings and the prominence of tapping in the occupational profile. The selection was based on the benchmark data available with the State Planning Board (Panchayat Development Reports) and discussions with key resource persons. The Panchayats selected for the study are Koottikkal, Parathodu and Mundakkayam (all in Kanjirappally); Pangode, Nanniyode and Peringamala (all in Nedumangad) and Vengola, Mazhuvannoor and Rayamangalam (all in Perumbavoor).

Kanjirappally assumes importance in the rubber cultivation history of Kerala as the scientific rubber cultivation was first introduced in the region. The area is well known for professional cultivation of the crop characterised by the highest productivity and finest quality of produce. The region also witnessed an early fragmentation of holdings leading to large-scale emergence of small holding cultivation of rubber alongside bigger plantations. The small holding cultivation in the region acquired further momentum with the institutional intervention of Rubber Board in early 1980s under its *Rubber to Poor* programme, which aimed at benefiting large section of small cultivators (10 cents and above). In the three Panchayats selected for the study rubber cultivation was found central. As per estimates collected from various issues of *Panchayat Vikasana Rekha* (Panchayat Development Reports) in Parathodu, the area under rubber accounted for more than 94 per cent of the total cultivated area, while in Mundakkayam and Koottikkal, this proportion was 83 per cent and 78 per cent respectively. The other major crops in the locality were mixed cropping of coconut, arecanut, pepper, tapioca and plantain. On the whole in all these panchayats, rubber tapping and other work in rubber gardens was the major farm based occupation. Among the non-farm occupations construction work was reported as the major engagement in the Panchayats.

Though rubber holdings are present in Nedumangad region for almost 60 years, the region is known for unprofessional approach in rubber cultivation. Unscientific approaches in rubber farming include, increased density of trees per acre, practicing of frequent and immature tapping, near absence of rain guarding and so on. In the selected three Panchayats of Nedumangad, rubber was found to occupy important position in agriculture. The proportion of area under rubber to the total cropped area is highest in Pangode (48 per cent), which was followed by Peringamala (33 per cent), and Nanniyode (24 per cent2). The major other agricultural crops in the region are coconut, paddy, arecanut, plantain, and vegetables. Apart from agricultural work, a few non-farm activities such as mat weaving, construction, quarry and brickklin work are also found in the region. As the locality is lying adjacent to Palode Reserve Forest Region and away from urban centres, such as Thiruvananthapuram, opportunities for wage work were found low.

In the Perumbavoor region rubber cultivation has only a short history of less than 40 years. However, the crop occupies an important position in the agriculture profile of the region. The proportion of area under rubber to the total cropped area is highest in Rayamangalam (31 per cent), which is followed by Vengola (27 per cent) and Mazhuvannoor (23 per cent). The major other agricultural crops in the region are paddy, coconut, pineapple, and pepper. The proximity to Perumbavoor town, a major trading centre in Ernakulam district provides several non-farm employment opportunities, especially in transportation and packaging activities.

The primary unit of data collection was tappers, who are engaged in the regular activity of tapping. In an operational sense, apart from cutting the trees, tapping include a range of activities such as removal of coagula, collection and transportation of latex and coagula, and sheet preparation. The scope of the study was limited to tappers in the small holdings. As per the definition followed by the Rubber Board, small holdings are plots with less than 20 hectares of land. However, in the study region, most of the plots are found falling under the category of less than 5 acres of land.

No reliable estimates on the number of tappers in the regions were available. The only source of information available on the number of tappers in these regions was the data with the Rubber Producers Societies. Rubber Producers Societies are micro level institutions registered under Societies Registration Act with voluntary participation from small growers under the aegis of Rubber Board with a view to promote improved farming practices and evolve group marketing strategies. The major limitation of the data with RPS is the non-availability of information regarding those tappers in small holding, which are not registered in these Societies. However, in the absence of other sources of information, the data with the RPS was used as the population for the selection of sample tappers. From each of the study regions, 120 tappers were selected randomly for the detailed study. Thus, the total sample size was 360 tappers employed in small holdings. These respondents were found engaged in 595 plots. Plot-wise information was gathered on important variables such as employment, wages, nature of contracts, extra wage supports and so on. Apart from employment data, household details were also collected to understand the coping strategies and livelihood diversification of tapper households. A pre-tested questionnaire was administered to gather information on household and personal details of the tapper, as well as various aspects of employment, wages, earnings and labour relations across plots (Annexure I). This information was supplemented through detailed discussions with select tappers as well as key informants such as trade union leaders, officials of Rubber Board and labour department, social activists, rubber traders and other workers in the study areas. In addition to this, detailed discussions were held with select growers from the study areas, primarily to gather additional information on contractual arrangements, cost of cultivation and land use pattern. A questionnaire was also administered among 60 growers who were selected giving adequate attention to the proportion of different size classes within small-holding sector (Annexure II).

The period of conducting the field study (2000-2002) also assumes importance as it coincided an acute product market crisis in the rubber sector, which commenced in 1996[17] and is believed to have resulted in the deterioration of labour welfare profile and conditions of work of the tappers-including non-revision of wages for years, denial of employment security and welfare benefits and waning of trade unionism.

Towards a Framework

In small holding farming, the major factors that underlie labour contracts are the problems of non-observability and non-enforceability of the work-effort of labour. In small farms because of imperfect information on work-effort of labour and the resultant costly supervision, the employer cannot, in most cases, specify and enforce the desired level of output. Further, because of the immeasurable effect of certain other factors on production, it becomes impossible to verify whether the lower output is due to the shirking of labour. This force the cultivators to adopt several risk aversion strategies including development of personal ties and provision of extra contractual benefits that covers moral hazard problems. While in industrial organisation, the enforceability of contract is attempted through incentive and penalty provisions, in agrarian set-up, especially in small farming this is done through establishment of personal ties. The need for nurturing personal relationships encourage the development of long term contracts interlinked with credit and insurance agreements. The framework of 'Agency Theory' or 'Principal-Agent Relationship' developed by Harris and Raviv (1978, 1979), Holmstorm (1979) and Shavell (1979)[18] could be used as a tool in the understanding of such dyadic relationships and the resultant risk sharing contractual arrangements in small holding cultivation.

An agency problem arises when the agent's action (work effort) is not directly observable by the principal and the outcome is influenced not only by the effort of the agent's action but also by certain factors beyond agent's control. In this context, the principal is not in a position to ensure whether the poor outcome is due to agent's idleness or unfavourable state of nature. This provides the scope for the agent to work less hard than the principal would like. However, if the agent's income is dependent upon the output of his effort, there is an incentive for him/her to work efficiently. The defect with this arrangement is that it renders the agent's income variable because the product of work depends not only on his/her action, but also on factors beyond his/her control. Being risk averse, an agent prefers a definite income to an indefinite income. Thus, as per the agency theory, the optimum contract seeks a balance between providing work incentives for the agent and lessening his exposure to risk.

Agency problem could also happen when the principal lacks perfect information on the agent's action. As the former's income is directly related to the work-effort of the latter, there arises a conflict between the contracting parties. The principal wants the agent to work harder, whereas work-effort generates disutility to the agent. Because of the imperfect information on the agents' work effort, the principal cannot specify and enforce the desired level of effort. Moreover, because of the immeasurable effect on production by uncertain factors, the principal cannot verify whether low output is due to the agent's shirking or due to unfavourable external factors. Thus, the agent is assumed to choose an action so as to maximize the (expected) utility given the structure of reward function, while the principal also selects a reward function that maximizes (expected) utility. In addition, in order to attract the agent, the principal must guarantee a utility not less than the reservation (or opportunity) utility of the agent (i.e., the agent's best available utility from a contract with some other principal or some other activity).

The first condition of agency problem is the non-observability of agent's effort by the principal, which *inter alia* determines the latter's pay off. It is postulated that small holding agriculture, in certain circumstances—not always—assume the characteristic of an agency problem. Observability of agent's (worker's) effort is possible in small farms if it is an intermittent operation, where the employer (principal) could easily observe the work or output and quantify on the work-effort. This removes all sort of casual and irregular operations in small farming from the purview of our analysis. A farmer could monitor the work-effort of the worker, even in regular operations, so long as the incremental returns (due to monitoring) is not less than opportunity income. However, in small holding situations, quite often, the opportunity income of the farmer far exceeds the incremental returns. Also, the small size of farm makes it too unviable to reap scale economies in monitoring the enforceability of the contract—for instance, engaging a supervisor. In large-scale holdings, as in the case of estate sector in plantations, the issue is non-existent as the employer could operate with scale economies, which enable engagement of supervisors and managers with lesser cost as in the case of industrial firms. In addition to this, there could also be situations when the principal is not in a position to attribute a loss/fall in production solely to the laziness or incompetence of the worker. Thus, it could be summed up that the small farming assumes the features of an agency problem, when the work is regular in nature, where the landlord is not in a position to monitor the contract directly (due to his higher opportunity income elsewhere), and where there are exogenous factors in determining the output.

As the principal's income is directly related to the agent's work effort, the former is bound to seek solutions for the aforesaid agency problem, despite the disadvantages of imperfect information. One way of tackling the issue is creating a system, which provides incentives (the best of which is higher wages) for the worker to exert more and to deter himself/herself from shirking—an endogenous solution. The second means is to build up a relationship between landlords and labour, which binds them vertically through ties of mutual obligations and duties. The latter approach emphasises the possibilities of a system of patronage where organising ideals of the system is based on a norm of reciprocity, in terms of mutualities, equivalent exchange of services, cooperation and independence (Bhattacharya, 2004).

Agency problems also occur when the principal is not familiar with the characteristics (e.g., ability) of the agent, which gives rise to the so-called adverse selection problem. The principal is willing to offer high remuneration only to the agent with suitable ability, because this contributes to increase output and, hence, the principal's income, whereas the agent attempts to choose that contract, which maximizes his utility with his ability. The problem for the principal here is to devise a set of contracts, which will induce the desired selection of contracts by agents. This personalisation of contracts allows both the parties to trade off with their opposing objects to reach non-market equilibrium, which involve commitments beyond contractual terms. In agrarian communities, the personal ties, however, are found adversely affecting the labour, especially as a constraint that prevents the organisation of workers through trade unions and institutionalisation of employment relations.

In view of the specific features of rubber tapping, characterised by unique work processes and timing of operations, the framework of agency theory could be used as a tool to disentangle the underlying dynamics of employment relations in small scale rubber holdings.

Hypotheses under Examination

In the subsequent chapters, while examining the employment, wages and labour relations in small holding sector, validity of a set of hypotheses is also examined. These hypotheses are:

(i) Due to the unique nature of labour requirement and labour process in small holding rubber tapping, the sector exhibits distinctive set of labour relations *vis-à-vis*, the rest of the agricultural occupations.

(ii) The unique nature of contractual arrangements and labour tying mechanisms in the small holding rubber sector lead to a situation, where the wages in the sector exhibit a different pattern of movement, as compared to the general wage trends in the rural sector as a whole.

(iii) The contractual arrangements and labour tying mechanisms in the small holdings are largely characterised by the presence of extra-wage supports and non-pecuniary benefits.

(iv) The workers in the small holding rubber plantations are less mobilised and organised under trade unions, unlike their counterparts in the estate sector and in other rural occupations.

(v) The coverage of governmental intervention through welfare programmes and protective legislations are minimal in the sector, due to the unique pattern of work organisation in the sector.

NOTES

1. Rubber cultivation in Kerala/India on a commercial scale is said to have commenced in 1902, when an Irish man, John Joseph Murphy, raised a rubber plantation in Thattekad, around 30 km. away from Cochin, with seeds imported from Ceylon (Government of India, 1968; Kurein, 2001).
2. The increased yield of rubber in the state can be attributed to factors such as favourable agro-climatic environment, commercialised farming and observance of scientific methods of planting and tapping.
3. For instance, the first rubber plantation in the state was of the area of 500 acres (202 hectares) (Government of India, 1968).
4. A major portion of the rubber production goes into tyre manufacture. Tyre Industry was in full-scale operation during the war period due to escalating demands from the war front.
5. Rubber to the Poor was a specific intervention programme launched by the Rubber Board to extend rubber cultivation to sub-marginal holders (with 10-50 cents).
6. Tapping rest is followed to increase the yield of the trees.
7. The average annual labour requirement in the small holding sector is estimated to be 160 days per ha. (Burger *et al.*, 1995); whereas in estate sector, it is 180 days per ha. (Pothen *et al.*, 2000).
8. The labour absorption capacity of Natural Rubber is estimated to be considerable lower as compared to other prominent crops, especially paddy, in Kerala.
9. The life of a rubber tree can be broadly divided into two: immature phase, which denotes the unproductive years, normally spanning 7-8 years; and the mature (harvesting) phase, which is the yielding period spanning to 20-25 years.
10. In some cases this may exceed more than 500 trees.
11. As drying of sheets in smoke houses involve some cost in terms of fuel wood, full fledged smoke houses are used commonly by

comparatively better off farmers. During rainy season, resource poor growers either dries the sheets by hanging it near the chimney of the kitchen or sells semi dried sheets at a lower price to traders who have facility to dry sheets. Some farmers also sell latex directly to the traders.

12. During rainy season also, tapping can be continued, fixing polythene rain-guard to the trunk above the tapping cut. About 35-40 additional tapping could be obtained every year by rain guarding the trees.
13. In the study regions the trees are given about 4-6 weeks rest during December-February, which is for increasing the lactating period.
14. The quantum of tapping (tapping task) available in a garden is generally denoted in terms of block, which denotes 300 trees. Normally, tapping of a block of trees would imply the engagement of an average worker for about 8 hours. However, according to the variations in the skill and experience, a block in the operational sense ranges between 300-400 trees.
15. Slaughter tapping is the intensive tapping generally done on old rubber trees for a few years prior to their removal. The methods employed for intensive tapping are increased tapping frequency, extension of tapping cut, opening of double cuts and use of yield stimulants.
16. Three states were included in the study and the field work related to the state of Kerala had been carried out fully by the author.
17. The market price of natural rubber reached it peak in 1995. From November 1996 onwards, it started declining drastically such that within the next five years the price got almost halved.
18. The Agency theory was developed drawing on the assumptions common to several representative theories of share tenancy advanced by Cheung, 1969; Bardhan and Srinivasan, 1971 and Stiglitz, 1974. Detailed discussion on the theory could be seen in Binswanger and Rosenswieg, 1984; Arrow, 1985; Levinthal, 1988; and Hayami and Otsuka, 1993.

5

Employment, Wages and Earnings in Small Holdings

Natural rubber cultivation occupies a pivotal position in Kerala's agriculture economy in terms of area and employment generation. The crop occupies the second position next to coconut, with a relative share of more than 16 per cent of the total cropped area. Of this, small holding sector occupies for more than 90 percentage of the area and generates an annual employment of around 39 million mandays (Viswanathan, *et al.* 2003), of which tapping accounts for 84 percentage of the labour requirement during the mature phase (Berger *et al.*, 1995).

Yet another major outcome of the organisational transformation in rubber farming is the emergence and growth of part-time farming, with considerable dependence on hired labour[1]. This increased dependence on hired labour is a marked departure from the initial phases of development of rubber cultivation in the state, which was characterised by intensive involvement of family labour in routine farm-management processes. The proliferation of small holdings along side part-time farming resulted in a large scale reporting of shortage of skilled rubber tappers, which was a core area of concern in small holdings, especially since the late 1980s and throughout the 1990s. As rubber tapping is a skilled occupation, a new entrant would take some time to establish as a tapper. Thus, always, there has been a lag associated with the entry of a tapper to the labour market. Considering these labour market implications, it is important to understand the dynamics of labour relations in rubber small holdings in the broader context of the state's rural labour market.

In the above backdrop, the discussion in the present chapter focuses on the aspects of employment, wages, earnings, organisation and welfare of tappers in the small holding sector. The analysis is based on the data collected from 360 tappers, a brief profile of whom is provided subsequently.

Profile of Tappers

The demographic and social profile of the respondents indicates certain interesting patterns (Table 5.1). The sex-wise segregation of the respondents reveals strikingly skewed distribution of workforce, with considerably lower participation of women, in all the study areas. This pattern of

Table 5.1: Profile of the Workers

	Perumbavoor	*Kanjirappally*	*Nedumangad*	*Total*
Sex				
Male	115 (95.8)	113 (94.2)	116 (96.7)	344 (95.6)
Female	5 (4.2)	7 (5.8)	4 (3.3)	16 (4.4)
Age				
<20	4 (3.3)	—	1 (0.8)	5 (1.4)
20-30	34 (28.4)	13 (10.8)	39 (32.5)	86 (23.9)
30-40	31 (25.8)	48 (40.0)	41 (34.2)	120 (33.3)
40-50	31 (25.8)	41 (34.2)	26 (21.7)	98 (27.2)
50-60	15 (12.5)	15 (12.5)	11 (9.2)	41 (11.4)
>60	5 (4.2)	3 (2.5)	2 (1.6)	10 (2.8)
Religion				
Hindu	83 (69.2)	68 (56.7)	75 (62.5)	226 (62.8)
Christian	31 (25.8)	37 (30.8)	17 (14.2)	85 (23.6)
Muslim	6 (5.0)	15 (12.5)	28 (23.3)	49 (13.6)
Caste				
FC	54 (45.0)	77 (64.2)	37 (30.8)	168 (46.7)
OBC	28 (23.3)	27 (22.5)	54 (45.0)	109 (30.3)
SC/ST	38 (31.7)	16 (13.3)	29 (24.2)	83 (23.0)
Education				
Illiterate	2 (1.7)	1 (0.8)	1 (0.8)	4 (1.1)
Upto Secondary	76 (63.3)	108 (90.0)	65 (54.2)	249 (69.2)
Secondary and Above	42 (35.0)	11 (9.2)	54 (45.0)	107 (29.7)

Source: Survey Data.
Note: Figures in parentheses are percentages to respective totals.

preponderance of male tappers was similar across study regions. Out of the 360 respondents surveyed, 96 per cent were men. A probing into the poor participation of women in the occupation reveal the 'invisible participation' of women, in about one-third of the cases. Quite often, the male tappers were found supported by female members and even children of the family. The male tappers get considerable assistance from their family members for collecting the latex and coagula, transportation of latex and preparation of rubber sheets. Usually, the male tapper starts tapping in the early hours of the day and the women and children were found joining the work with a lag of two-three hours. Here, though the work is carried out collectively, the contributions of women and children remain invisible, as they are neither recognised nor remunerated as assistants[2]. The lower absorption of women labour in rubber holdings has been cited as a major issue in the development discourse of the state, especially during 1970s, with the commendable increase in the area under the crop at the cost of female labour intensive crops such as paddy[3].

The patterns of age-wise distribution are found similar across the regions. Most of the tappers are concentrated in the age group of 20-50 (84.4 per cent). Within this category, the concentration is more in the age group of 30-45 (60.5 per cent).

The participation was negligible below 20 years and above 60 years. The lower participation of youngsters in tapping could be partly attributed to the late entry into the occupation due to the skilled nature of job[4] and the aversion among rural households in undertaking agricultural operations. Though tapping is found to be a comparatively preferred job against other farm works, its acceptability was affected considerably due to massive fall in price of natural rubber and the resultant stagnation in wages. The absence of elderly could be attributed to the manually demanding nature of the occupation. It was observed that due to physical exertion many tappers find it difficult to continue tapping for long years, which is evident in the survey, where none of the respondents has work experience of more than 30 years[5].

Majority of workers (62.8 per cent) were Hindus, followed by Christians (23.6 per cent) and Muslims (13.6 per cent). The pattern was slightly different in Nedumangad, where Muslims assumed the second place (23.3 per cent). Majority of tappers belonged to upper castes (46.7 per cent)[6]. The higher level of participation of backward and upper castes in the occupation is distinct from the traditional social ordering, where those who belong to lowest rungs of caste system are mostly engaged in agricultural operations. Tapping is a comparatively new rural occupation, which does not fit into any of the socially reserved categories for workers belonging to lower rungs of the caste hierarchy. The caste free identity of the job attracts people from upper castes to accept it, as it is not 'demeaning' to their social status. People from the socially backward castes also prefer tapping, as it helps them to come out of the grips of caste hierarchy[7]. This needs to be seen in a broader context of the widely documented aversion of Keralites to accept 'blue collar' jobs[8]. The general acceptance of the occupation, cutting across the caste hierarchies indicates that the shying away of Kerala labour from farm operations is determined by the social status attached to the job within the caste hierarchy.[9]

Most of the respondents were literates (about 99 per cent). Around 30 per cent was found to have education level of secondary and above. This pattern, however, is not same across regions. While 45 per cent of workers in Nedumangad have education above SSLC, in Perumbavoor and Kanjirappally their proportions were 35 and 9.2 per cent, respectively. The lower educational status among the tappers of Kanjirappally can be linked to the higher presence of elderly among the workers.

About 55 per cent of the tappers had at least 0.30 acre of land planted with rubber (with an average holding size of 0.45 ha), which in turn suggest that majority of the workers are also petty growers. The status of land ownership as well as higher share of area under rubber make the tappers a distinct category of labourers, in contrast to the predominance of marginal and landless labourers in general agriculture of the state (Viswanathan *et al.*, 2003). The proportion of migrant workers was very low (5 per cent) and all these migrant tappers were working in Kanjirappally. The region has reported to be experiencing shortage of skilled tappers since mid 1980s. The major pockets of origin of migrant workers are Thiruvananthapuram district of Kerala and Kanyakumari district of Tamil Nadu. The presence of migrant workers is attributed to a number of factors including, increase in number of holdings and small growers; increased educational status and the changed aspirations of youth in the locality; increased availability of alternative occupations; and a general enhancement in the standard of living, mainly due to the prosperity arising out of rubber cultivation and trade.

Employment Implications of Small-Scale Farming

The sub-division and fragmentation of rubber farms, have been unique compared to other plantation crops and has given rise to various agro-management issues with serious implications in the labour market. The employment prospects of the sector are cumulatively determined by the pattern of tapping and the level of tapping task. As discussed earlier, the major patterns of tapping in the small holdings could be divided into three: D/1, D/2 and D/3. In the survey, of the 595 plots, 72 per cent of tappers were found working with D/2 system, which is followed by D/1 pattern (25 per cent). Perumbavoor and Kanjirappally had shown almost similar pattern in the diffusion of D/2 pattern with an incidence level of 89 per cent and 96 per cent respectively. As against this, Nedumangad had D/1 pattern in 84 per cent cases (Table 5.2). This increased level of incidence of D/1 pattern in Nedumangad may be attributed to several reasons including lower productivity and profitability of the crop especially due to geo-climatical conditions. Compared to the other study areas, the growers in the region are found to be economically backward. The status of full time farming, smaller size of plots, low productivity of the crop and the distant location of the area from trading centres are found to force farmers to entertain a short-run approach to farming. The low economic status of farmers in the region is further evident from the reported instances of sale of semi-dried sheets and even latex itself to the traders.

Table 5.2: Distribution of Plots across Patterns of Tapping

System of Tapping	*Perumbavoor*	*Kanjirappally*	*Nedumangad*	*Total*
D/1	19 (7.5)	8 (4.1)	124 (83.8)	151 (25.4)
D/2	225 (89.3)	187 (95.9)	20 (13.5)	432 (72.6)
D/3	8 (3.2)	—	4 (2.7)	12 (2.0)
Total	252 (100.0)	195 (100.0)	148 (100.0)	360 (100.0)

Source: Survey data.
Note: Figures in parentheses are percentages to respective totals.

The survey data suggests that the small holdings in Kerala are characterised by inadequate availability of tapping task. Given the prominence of D/2 tapping pattern in the study regions, to ensure employment for a tapper on regular basis, the minimum required tapping task is 600 trees. An examination of the plot-wise details (Table 5.3) shows that the average number of trees per acre differ across regions with Kanjirappally having the lowest intensity of cropping with 120 trees per acre followed by Nedumangad (202 trees) and Perumbavoor (236 trees)[10]. A closer examination of the plot-wise details reveals that irrespective of the study regions, the average tapping task was found too low to employ a tapper throughout the year.

Table 5.3: Details of Plots and Average Tapping Task

Characteristics	*Perumbavoor*	*Kanjirappally*	*Nedumangad*	*Total*
No. of plots	252	195	148	595
Average plot size (in acre)	1.2	3.2	2.0	2.0
Average number of trees per acre	235.6	120.2	201.5	168.0
Average tapping task per plot (no. of trees)	251.0	378.8	271.7	294.0

Source: Survey data.

As discussed earlier, the prominent pattern of tapping followed in Perumbavoor and Kanjirappally is D/2. Given the average tapping task in these regions as 251 and 379 respectively, it is evident that most of the tappers are not in a position to ensure adequate employment from a single plot. In Perumbavoor, the situation is more severe where a worker gets an average tapping task of only 251 trees, which is much below the required minimum for a day's work (300 trees). Existence of reduced tapping task is also true in the case of Nedumangad (271 trees) despite the prevalence of D/1 tapping.

Multiple Grower Dependency and its Employment Connotations

The lower quantum of tapping task available from small holdings makes it impossible for the tapper to realise a reasonable level of employment from a single holder. To address this situation, the tappers were found attaching themselves with more than one grower. In all the study regions, this 'multiple grower dependency' was visible with some degree of inter-area variations. A considerable proportion of the respondents (54 per cent) were found employed in more than one plot (Table 5.4).

Table 5.4: Distribution of Tappers according to Number of Plots Attended

Categories	*Perumbavoor*	*Kanjirappally*	*Nedumangad*	*Total*
One Grower	35 (29.2)	36 (30)	94 (78.3)	165 (45.8)
Two Growers	40 (33.3)	83 (69.2)	21 (17.5)	144 (40.0)
Three Growers	45 (37.5)	1 (0.8)	5 (4.2)	51 (14.2)
Total	120 (100.0)	120 (100.0)	120 (100.0)	360 (100.0)

Source: Survey data.
Note: Figures in parentheses are percentages to respective totals.

As D/2 pattern of tapping was more prominent in Perumbavoor and Kanjirappally, it is understandable that reliance on multiple holdings is inevitable in these study regions. In both Perumbavoor and Kanjirappally, about 70 per cent of the tappers were attached to more than one employer, while in Perumbavoor the situation was more pronounced with about 38 per cent of workers in triple employer status.

Nedumangad, however, showed a totally different pattern where 78 per cent of respondents were working with single growers. The reasons for these interregional differences are the variation in terms of average size of holdings and the pattern of tapping. On the whole, the situation is that of a tapper, simultaneously engaged in different plots in a single day or during alternative days, which is a marked departure from the conventional system of labour relations in rubber holdings.

Simultaneous engagement in multiple plots thus could be understood as a means to earn a reasonable level of daily wage income through ensuring a critical minimum of tapping task. In situations of reliance on multiple growers, tappers are found either working on more than one plots on a particular day or engaged in different plots on different days of D/2 or D/3 pattern of tapping. This phenomenon of multiple employer status, *prima facie,* could be viewed as situation of enhanced vulnerability and footloose situation of the workforce. Nevertheless, there are ample reasons to believe that in rural labour markets, which are characterised by labour shortage in general, this multiple-employer status adds to the bargaining power (reservation wage) of the worker. The worker enjoys certain level of freedom, as s/he is not solely dependent on a single employer. This freedom adds to the bargaining power of the worker, which in turn reflects in favourable contractual parameters.

The number of days of employment was found inadequate even with reliance on multiple growers, which is evident from the data on the combined tapping task per tapper. Majority of the tappers (77 per cent) are faced with the problem of inadequate tapping task, (Table 5.5), given the prominence of D/2 pattern of tapping. This shows the extent of underemployment prevailing among tappers.

A correlation between combined tapping task and years of experience of tapper showed significant and positive coefficients in the case of Kanjirappally (0.722) and Perumbavoor (0.594), which is suggestive of a situation where higher levels of experience lead to increased work availability.

However, Nedumangad stood apart from this pattern with a negative coefficient (–0.371), which could be attributed to the widespread prevalence of D/1 tapping with lower levels of tapping task per operational holdings.

Table 5.5: Region-wise Distribution of Tappers according to Combined Tapping Task

Tapping task (No. of trees)	*Perumbavoor*	*Kanjirappally*	*Nedumangad*	*Total*
Upto 300	10 (8.3)	21 (17.5)	9 (7.5)	40 (11.1)
300-400	27 (22.5)	21 (17.5)	45 (37.5)	93 (25.8)
400-500	17 (14.2)	25 (20.8)	28 (23.3)	70 (19.4)
500-600	47 (39.2)	18 (15.0)	8 (6.7)	73 (20.3)
Above 600	19 (15.8)	35 (29.2)	30 (25.0)	84 (23.3)
Total	120 (100)	120 (100)	120 (100)	360 (100)

Source: Survey data.
Note: Figures in parentheses are percentages to respective totals

The distribution of tappers as per employment days further reveals the intensity of unemployment. Only 43.6 per cent of respondents were found getting more than 6 months' employment from tapping (Table 5.6). The region-wise disaggregation of the data however shows totally different patterns. For instance, in Perumbavoor only 5 per cent of

Table 5.6: Distribution of Tappers across Average Number of Days of Employment Per Year

No. of days of employment	*Perumbavoor*	*Kanjirappally*	*Nedumangad*	*Total*
Upto 120	8 (6.7)	3 (2.5)	1 (0.8)	12 (3.3)
121-150	74 (61.7)	16 (13.3)	4 (3.3)	94 (26.1)
151-180	32 (26.7)	10 (8.3)	55 (45.8)	97 (26.9)
181-210	5 (4.2)	32 (26.7)	57 (47.5)	94 (26.1)
211-240	—	24 (20.0)	2 (1.7)	26 (7.2)
241 and above	1 (0.8)	35 (29.2)	1 (0.8)	37 (10.3)
Total	120 (100.0)	120 (100.0)	120 (100.0)	360 (100.0)

Source: Survey data.
Note: Figures in parentheses are percentages to respective totals.

workers are found to have employment for more than 6 months. These proportions are 50 per cent and 75.9 per cent in Nedumangad and Kanjirappally respectively. While the higher level of tapping days in Kanjirappally could be attributed to the increased use of rain guarded tapping[11], the better picture of Nedumangad is due to the preponderance of D/1 tapping.

Lower tapping task would also lead to division of labour and specialisation in select process(es). In some of the tiny holdings the tappers were found confining their work strictly to the process of cutting the bark[12], leaving the subsequent operations to the growers themselves. Several tappers find this arrangement suitable, considering the lesser time required per holding. Quite often, the growers too prefer this arrangement, as it enables them to productively utilise the available family labour in the post-tapping operations, thereby reducing the overall labour costs[13].

Wages and Earnings

The tapping task along with quantum of employment and wage rate determines the level of earnings of the tappers. In contrast to the estate sector[14], the wage payment system in small holdings is based on piece rates. The wages are normally expressed as payment per tree or as payment per block[15]. In the survey 95.56 per cent of the tappers were found employed solely with piece rate wage contracts[16]. While the piece rate wages was prominent in Perumbavoor (93 per cent) and Nedumangad (96 per cent) in Kanjirappally, the prevalence of the system was complete. The rest of the tappers (14 cases—8 in Perumbavoor; and 6 in Nedumangad), were found engaged in output contracts (product sharing) as a conditionally accepted system, in which the growers and tappers share sheets or income from sale of sheets, mostly on a 50 : 50 basis. This system is a recent development and could be attributed to the crisis in rubber market. In all the cases of product sharing, it was found that tiny holders (with less than 75 cents) have gone for product sharing arrangements due to their inability to advance wages to tappers.

Small holding tappers come under the provisions of Minimum Wage Act, 1948. As per the Act, as on 31-03-2001 minimum piece rate wage for tapping 100 trees is Rs. 25.9. The actual wage rates in the study regions ranged between Ps. 18-35. While Perumbavoor and Kanjirappally showed more or less similar pattern of wages, with more than 85 per cent of the tappers paid within a range of Ps. 26-35 per tree. The wages in Nedumangad were the lowest—with 95 per cent of tappers paid below Ps. 26 per tree (Table 5.7)[17].

Table 5.7: Distribution of Tappers based on Per Tree Wage Rates

Category	*Perumbavoor*	*Kanjirappally*	*Nedumangad*	*Total*
Not applicable	8 (6.7)	—	6 (5.0)	14 (3.9)
Upto 20 paise	1 (0.8)	—	89 (74.2)	90 (25.0)
21-25 paise	5 (4.2)	17 (14.2)	25 (20.8)	47 (13.1)
26-30 paise	86 (71.7)	74 (61.7)	—	160 (44.4)
Above 30 paise	20 (16.6)	29 (24.2)	—	49 (13.6)
Total	120 (100.0)	120 (100.0)	120 (100.0)	360 (100.0)

Source: Survey data.
Note: Figures in parentheses are percentages to respective totals.

Average wage rate was found to be Ps. 27 for all regions together. The higher wages in Kanjirappally could be attributed to the relative shortage of skilled tappers in the region. Further, it was reported that to ensure higher productivity and enhanced longevity of trees the growers retain skilled workers by paying more wages[18]. Yet another probable reason for the prevalence of higher wages is the region's proximity to the estate sector, where periodic wage revisions exist. It was highlighted that the frequent wage revisions in the estate sector provide some benchmark for wage revisions in the small holdings.

The higher wages in Perumbavoor could be partially attributed to the acute inadequacy in terms of tapping task, which in turn delimits the bargaining capacity of the employers (or enhances the stake of labour). Secondly, in Perumbavoor, the growers are found fixing the per tree wages at a higher level due to the higher reservation income of the workers, arising out of the comparatively higher availability of alternative job opportunities (especially due to the regions proximity to the Perumbavoor Town, a well known trading centre in the state). Further to this, the region is prominently characterised by part-time growers, who are not in a position to monitor the work-effort of the tapper, and thus are willing to pay slightly higher wages to ensure loyalty. The lower wages in Nedumangad could be attributed to a host of factors such as absence of alternative employment opportunities[19], the short-run approach of farmers towards rubber cultivation and the relatively lower profitability of rubber farming in the locality.

In some of the holdings, to tie the tappers, the growers were found giving higher piece rate wages. In certain cases, this is to ensure a reasonable level of wage income. Considering their inability to provide adequate tapping task to the worker and in view of their opportunity cost (wage income from alternative employment or from a bigger holding), the growers were found agreeing to some reasonable hike in the per tree wages. In some cases, the small holders were also found compensating those workers who spend considerable time on transit between the plots, so as to ensure them a fair level of earnings.

An examination of the correlation between tapping task and piece rate wages show significant and negative relationships, which was more prominent in Perumbavoor (–0.532) followed by Kanjirappally (–0.312) and Nedumangad (–0.105). This point towards a situation where tappers are given higher wages to compensate for the lower tapping task and *vice versa*, which broadly reflects the labour retaining mechanism adopted by small growers to counter skilled labour shortages.

As against the normal pattern of strong correspondence between workers' experience and wage rates in rural areas, the survey data did not show any strong correlation. Though the correlation coefficients between piece rate wages and the years of engagement in tapping were found positive, their values were below 0.4 in all regions. While Kanjirappally showed a better value of 0.380, in Perumbavoor and

Nedumangad the corresponding coefficients were 0.168 and 0.032 respectively.

Inadequate level of tapping task leading to reduced number of days of employment combined with lower piece rate wages cumulatively result in strikingly lower levels of daily wages earnings to the tappers (Table 5.8). Given the prominence of a system, where wages are paid on a per tree basis, the tappers' aim of ensuring a fair level of wage income could be met mainly through an assured level of tapping task. This compulsion, *inter alia*, forces the tappers to club tapping tasks from various plots so as to maintain a particular level of per day employment.

Table 5.8: Daily Wage Earnings from Piece Rate Tapping

	Perumbavoor	*Kanjirappally*	*Nedumangad*	*Total*
Not applicable	8 (6.7)	—	6 (5.0)	14 (3.9)
Upto Rs. 70	17 (14.2)	8 (6.7)	74 (61.7)	99 (27.5)
Rs. 71-80	14 (11.7)	18 (15.0)	29 (24.2)	61 (16.9)
Rs. 81-90	25 (20.8)	34 (28.3)	5 (4.2)	64 (17.8)
Rs. 91-100	12 (10.0)	17 (14.2)	3 (2.5)	32 (8.9)
Rs. 101-110	24 (20.0)	13 (10.8)	—	37 (10.3)
Rs. 111-120	15 (12.5)	18 (15.0)	1 (0.8)	34 (9.4)
Above Rs. 120	5 (4.2)	12 (10.0)	2 (1.7)	19 (5.3)
Total	120 (100.0)	120 (100.0)	120 (100.0)	360 (100.0)

Source: Survey data.
Note: Figures in parentheses are percentages to respective totals.

As shown in the Table, 71.01 per cent of the tappers were found receiving daily wage earnings less than or equal to Rs.100, during a tapping day. The proportion was highest in Nedumangad (91.6 per cent); it was 64.2 per cent and 60.7 per cent in Kanjirappally and Perumbavoor respectively. The fact that more than one-third of the workers in Kanjirappally and Perumbavoor earned more than Rs.100 wages, while in Nedumangad, their proportion was only 2.5 per cent.

The existence of low level daily wage earnings from piece rate tapping is quite contrary to the overall situation in the state, which is otherwise known for prevalence of higher wages across most of the rural occupations. A comparison of daily wage earnings from tapping with the daily wages in other rural occupations in the state would further clarify the lower level of wages in the sector. For instance, in 2001-2002, average daily wage rates of various categories of rural labour were: Carpenter: Rs. 185; Mason: Rs.185; Unskilled construction worker—Male Rs. 129; Female Rs. 106; Unskilled paddy field worker—Male: Rs. 126; Female Rs. 85 (Government of Kerala, 2002).

The average annual wage earnings per worker for all the regions were estimated as Rs. 15748, with considerable regional variations. While Kanjirappally showed a fairer picture with Rs. 20240, in Perumbavoor and Nedumangad, these figures were Rs. 14197 and Rs. 12543 respectively (Table 5.9).

Table 5.9: Average Annual Employment, Wages and Earnings Across Study Areas

Characteristics	*Perumbavoor*	*Kanjirappally*	*Nedumangad*	*Total*
Average annual wage earnings (in Rs.)*	14197.2	20240.2	12543.3	15748.1
Average annual employment days	153.1	208.8	183.9	181.9
Average daily wage earnings** (in Rs.)	92.6	96.9	68.2	85.1

Source: Survey data.

Note: * These figures are arrived at by dividing the average annual employment days.

** These figures are arrived at by dividing the average annual wage earnings by 365.

As seen before, the average employment figures also varied drastically across regions within a range of 153-209 and with an overall average of 182 days. The two implications of the aforesaid level of earnings and employment are: (a) the lower level of average daily earnings, which ranged between Rs. 68 and Rs. 97 in the study regions; and (b) the lower levels of daily per capita income accruing from tapping (which ranged between Rs. 33 and Rs. 55 across study regions). On the whole, the data is suggestive of the comparatively higher employment availability in tapping, despite a low level of daily wage earnings from the occupation. The reasonably high level of annual wage earnings underlines the significance of the occupation.

Stagnation in Wages

Wages in all the study regions are reported to have almost stagnated or even declined for about a period of 5-6 years. This trend in wages is mainly linked to the crisis in the domestic natural rubber market, consequent to its integration with world natural price movements since the mid 1990s. Before the onset of the crisis, wages in tapping have registered continuous increase owing to the close linkage between product prices and wages. For instance, in Kanjirappally, during the period 1990-92, the rising tendency of natural rubber caused a marked rise in wages by 33 per cent bringing the average wage rate from Rs. 18 to Rs. 24 per 100 trees. During 1994-95 wages rates rose to Rs. 30 per 100 trees. Subsequently due to fluctuations in international rubber prices, wage rates started declining (Ushadevi and Jayachandran, 2001). The stagnation in wages in tapping could be seen from the perspective of rising wages in alternative rural occupations and the cost of living of the workers. The real wages of agricultural work and casual work in construction have shown an increase of 35 per cent during the period 1990 to 2000 (Mahesh, 2002). Thus, it is quite evident that in the recent period, the relative wages of tapping *vis-à-vis* the wages of alternative rural occupations have gone down considerably.

The fact that workers are found sticking to tapping even with comparatively low daily wage earnings warrants further probing into the probable factors that make the occupation attractive. Firstly, as evident from the employment data, though the average number of employment days available are not too high, it is comparatively better than the quantum of employment available in other farm operations. For instance, coconut and paddy are found generating not less than 80 and 120 days of average number of annual employment, respectively. The comparatively low degree of uncertainty in employment is another dimension that makes employment in rubber tapping appealing. The availability of certain and continuous employment for a greater part of the year makes rubber tapping economically attractive *vis-à-vis* other agricultural and rural operations.

The flexibility attached to tapping is yet another attraction of the occupation. It is possible for a tapper to complete the tapping operations and then take up casual work elsewhere during the same day. The caste free identity of the job also add to the desirability of tapping even when the wages are relatively lower compared to those jobs which are positioned according to the caste-based social hierarchy. For instance, the farm operations such as toddy tapping, coconut plucking and paddy operations are highly caste based occupations and hence do not come in the choice matrix of many of the tappers who prefer to maintain a caste free label in the labour market.

Another possible reason, which deters the mobility of tappers from the occupation, is the 'skill trap' imposed by continued engagement in tapping. Tappers consider tapping as a highly skilled occupation and hence moving to other farm operations and unskilled rural operations would imply a downward movement. At the same time, many of the elderly tappers find it difficult to get absorbed in other skilled occupations as they lack minimum technical know-how and abilities required in these fields due to their long engagement in tapping.

Contrary to the inertia among the elderly tappers to switch over from the occupation, the unimpressive wage profile of tapping is reported to have affected the influx of younger generations into the occupation. Most of the respondents do not want their children to join the occupation. Further, young tappers reported that they consider tapping as a temporary livelihood arrangement within the bleak employment situation in rural areas. The increased tendency among youngsters to move to alternative occupations has reported leading to high turnover rates and a subsequent shortage of skilled tappers in the study regions. This was more prominent in Kanjirappally, where growers reported shortage skilled local hands and are forced to engage migrant labour from other regions.

The foregoing discussion underlines three important aspects of labour market dynamics of tappers in the study regions, such as: (a) small size of operational holdings leading to inadequate levels of tapping task and a resultant reliance on multiple growers; (b) existence of lower levels of piece rate wages with comparatively better employment potential cumulatively leading to comparable levels of annual wage earnings *vis-à-vis* other rural occupations; and (c) the stagnating trend of wages which lead to an emerging situation of shortage of skilled labour in the sector.

The analysis is suggestive of a continuum of developments, where structural changes in rubber holdings have resulted in a proliferation of small and marginal holdings affecting the level of employment, wages and earnings. It is evident that even with multiple grower dependence, the tappers are finding it difficult to get adequate levels of tapping task and year round employment in the rubber holdings. The resultant reduced average annual earnings, during a period of crisis in rubber markets, is found deterring the entry of younger generation into the occupation thereby leading to situations of shortage of skilled labour. Though the shortage is still in its nascent stage and to some extent could be attributed to the imperfect information and lack of coordination in rural areas, it is likely to become more acute, in view of the reduced preference of younger generation towards tapping on account of prevailing lower and stagnant wages.

Organisational Aspects: Trade Unionism among Tappers

The phenomenon of stagnating wages is surely an outlier in the overall scene of Kerala's labour market. This pattern could be attributed largely to the weak presence of trade unions in the sector. It was reported that the influence of trade unions among tappers has deteriorated considerably in recent years. For instance, majority of the respondents in the survey disowned the trade union movement and highlighted that tappers engaged in small holdings are normally excluded from the priorities of mainstream trade union movement. On the whole, across the study regions, the strength and relevance of trade unions are found waning. The organisational efforts among tappers by the trade unions have become minimal and, in most of the cases, confine to negotiations regarding compensation during times of retrenchment or felling of trees. None of the study regions do not have a recent history of organising a successful strike or any other visible form of worker protest.

An analysis of the trade union activities and mobilisation level of tappers reveals very interesting and unassuming findings. With certain variations in the characterisation and features, the influence of trade unions on tappers was found extremely marginal in the holding sector. Here, it needs to be noted that the tappers of estate sector in rubber plantation has been with a considerable level of organisational history. In none of the study regions, trade unions of tappers as such were not present. In the absence of separate union of tappers, some tappers were found to be members of generic trade unions affiliated to major political parties (such as CITU, AITUC and INTUC).

The participation of tappers in trade union activities was found lowest in Nedumangad, followed by Perumbavoor. In Nedumangad, majority of the workers are not even aware of the activities of trade unions in their locality. It is found that in the event of resolving any work-related issues, the tappers normally approach local leaders of various political parties[20]. Among the trade unions affiliated with various political parties in the region, CITU was found more prominent. Among the 120 respondents from the locality only 18 were members of some union. Out of these only 2 were found to be office bearers of trade unions, at least once, since their entry into tapping.

In Perumbavoor, though some trade unions under the aegis of political parties were present, their current activities and hold among tappers were not much prominent. Some tappers who are members of AITUC recollect that the union activities were successful in the 1970s and in the early 1980s, in bringing out wages revisions and benefits to the workers. The membership of tappers in AITUC for the entire Taluk is less than 70 now, where majority of these members are passive members or those who retain membership due to their overall political leaning. CITU, which has started its activities among the tappers around the early 1990s, has the maximum membership (around 300). The other trade union—INTUC, which started activities only in the late 1990s, do not have more than 20 members. Despite a dip in trade union activities in the recent past, a comparatively brighter picture in Perumbavoor could be attributed mainly to the overall political background of the region, where communist parties have a strong hold, in general.

In Kanjirappally, active involvement of tappers in trade union movement is almost absent with none of the respondents holding membership even in general trade unions affiliated to the political parties. It was pointed out that there is no need for any trade union activity in the small holding sector, since political parties are readily available to be approached, in times of support such as wage revision or a dispute resolution in case of retrenchment allowance.

Although all these regions exhibit poor organizational profiles, at present, it is found that trade unions were active during the 1970s and the 1980s in all these areas. During this period, the tappers recollect that, unions were successful in bringing frequent wage revisions through various strategies including organisation of token strikes and tripartite negotiations. However, since mid 1980s, the role of the trade union got shrunk to that of a mediator in the event of dispute settlement such as negotiating for compensation to the worker at the time of felling of trees or retrenchment. The status of trade unions has further deteriorated since mid 1990s, following the overall crisis in the rubber sector. During the period of a continuing price crash, tappers are fully aware that there is no point in collectively bargaining for a wage revision, which is simply unaffordable by the farmer. Thus, in recent times, even the negotiations are done or disputes are settled mutually between the farmers and tappers without involving trade unions.

There was a wider consensus among respondents across regions that the relevance of the trade unions has eroded considerably in the recent years. Most of the tappers view involvement in trade unions as wastage of money (towards membership and some nominal collections) and time, as the issues of tappers in small holdings do not find place in the priorities of mainstream trade union movement. The fact that Kanjirappally has higher wages, despite any trade union activity is also cited as an instance to narrate the irrelevance of trade unionism in the small holding sector. It was also held that trade unions do not have much role in wage revision, as compared to product price fluctuations.

There are ample evidences supporting the visible discontent among the tappers regarding the functioning of trade unions. The unions or leaders of unions are reported to be indulged in corruption and nepotism, according to most of the respondents, across the study regions. Even in Perumbavoor, where the workers are generally involved in political parties, this was highlighted as a serious issue. The arguments against trade unions include rent seeking by the political leaders and trade union leaders and undesirable nexus between the trade unions and the growers. Cases of union members giving bribe to settle their issues are also reported. In cases where the unions mediate the issues such as retrenchment compensation, normally, the tapper and the union leader/local politician would informally agree upon the share to the latter, from the compensation amount, which ranges between 10-20 per cent. The unions are often found misusing their bargaining power for attaining undue claims for the party members or for settling scores on other issues with individual cultivators. Further, the insensitivity of the trade union leaders or political parties in fighting the causes of tappers in the small holding sector is widely reported. Several reasons have been put forth for this disinterest and lack of enthusiasm, such as: (a) non-representation of tappers in the leadership; (b) limited scope for corruptive practices to the political leaders; and (c) the unique issues faced by the political parties in organising the workers in small holdings.

The substitution of the role of trade unions by political parties further complicates and deteriorates the relevance of the former. As political parties also include growers as the members or office bearers and as some of them are more powerful than the tappers within the party, in many a case, the settlements brings in favourable results to the growers only. This is specifically true in the case of Kanjirappally, where the rubber growers are the strong pillars of most of the political parties.

The increased aversion of tappers in organisational activities could partly be related to the fear of job loss. Many tappers believe that involvement in union activities would worsen their relationship with the growers and eventually leads to the termination of contractual ties. For instance, in cases where annual contracts are observed, tappers fear that the term would not be renewed, if the grower takes into note their involvement in trade union activities.

Legislative Protection and Welfare Measures

The labour in small and tiny rubber holdings (below 5 ha.) are out of the reach of the protective frame of the Plantation Labour Act of 1951, which defines 'plantation' as: *"any land used or intended to be used for growing tea, coffee, rubber, cinchona or cardamom which admeasures 5 hectares or more and in which fifteen or more persons are employed or were employed on any day of the preceding twelve months"* (Malik, 2003). During the survey, an increasing tendency is noticed among the growers to delimit the size of holdings below the cut of point of 5 ha. Though, the scope of the study is on those holdings below 20 hectares as per the definition of the Rubber Board, only one plot is found coming under this category of above 5 ha. From detailed probing, it is understood that most of the growers are keen in keeping their holding size below 5 ha. to circumvent the extra burden of providing the benefits stipulated under the Plantation Labour Act, 1951. It was noted that large holdings are shown as fragmented small holdings in paper, though it belonged to the same household and thus managed centrally, denying the tappers the benefits under the Plantation Labour Act, 1951.

The exclusion from the provisions of Plantation Labour Act, 1951 brings in a visible gap between the tapper in the unorganised small holding sector and their counterparts in the organised estate sector. The Act assures the workers reasonable amenities like supply of drinking water, suitable medical and educational facilities, canteen, crèches and sufficient latrines and urinals, separately for males and females. The Act also regulates the working hours and leave without wages of workers employed in plantations. Further to this, the tappers in the small and tiny holdings are deprived of a host of benefits stipulated under the other protective legislations, which are applicable to the workers in the estate sector and cover a multitude of aspects and conditions of labour including wage rates, dearness and other allowances, bonus, hours of work, overtime, leave, holidays with pay, residential accommodation, superannuation benefits (like gratuity, provident fund and pension), benefits related to grading, promotion, retirement and procedures for strike, lay-out and lay off.

The extent of welfare measures available to the tappers in small holdings is limited to the schemes provided by the Rubber Board (Table 5.10), in line with the stipulations of the Rubber Act, 1947, which provides amongst other functions that *'it shall be the duty of the Board to secure better working conditions and the provisions and improvement of amenities and incentives for rubber plantation workers'*. As per the stipulations of the Rubber Board, all these benefits are available to those small holding or tiny holding sector rubber tappers, who have been continuously working with a particular employer for a certain number of years. Accordingly, a certification from the employer is necessary for the tapper to avail these benefits from the Board. Notwithstanding these, during the survey, it is found that only a meagre proportion of the respondents have availed the benefits out of these welfare provisions, at least once. In most of the cases, it is noted that they fail to get the necessary certification from the employer. Most of the small and tiny growers are reported avoiding giving written documents that testify the workers' continuous involvement in the farm work. The growers fear that, given the history of Kerala's industrial relations, any written document from the employers might bring adverse results in the future, as it happened in the case of rendering land rights to attached tenants, during the land reforms of the 1970s. Further to this, it was also evident from the survey data that many of the `beneficiaries' of the schemes being offered by the Rubber Board do not have anything to do with tapping, as several of the claims were made by the relatives and dependants (friends and `trusted' persons) of the growers, who managed to obtain the required certification.

All these suggest that the rubber tappers in the small and tiny holding sector are not only deprived of the protective provisions of the Plantation Labour Act, 1951, but also subject to massive exclusion from otherwise legitimately eligible benefits from the Rubber Board. This situation, however, to a greater extent, is linked to lower bargaining power of the workers, in a crisis phase which is partly linked to the process of globalisation and its adverse impact on the product market of natural rubber.

Table 5.10: Labour Welfare Schemes of Rubber Board

Scheme	*Details*
Educational Stipend Scheme	This scheme is intended for payment of educational stipend comprising of tuition fee, hostel/boarding fee and lump sum grant (towards the purchase of books and instruments) to children of rubber plantation workers for pursuing studies in recognised courses.
Educational Scholarship Scheme	The scheme provides for grant of scholarship to children of workers who meritoriously pass examinations of recognised courses.

(contd.)

(TABLE 5.10 contd.)

Scheme	*Details*
Group Insurance-cum-Deposit-Scheme	The objective of the scheme is to encourage workers in the unorganised sector to develop the habit of saving on a long term basis and to cover them against accidents.As per the scheme a worker has to contribute a sum of Rs. 50 per year and the Board in turn will contribute Rs. 100 per worker per year. Out of this Rs. 150 an amount of Rs. 16 will be paid to insurance companies as premium for covering personal accident and the remaining Rs. 134 will be deposited in securities. The scheme is for a period of ten years and on maturity each worker will get an amount of Rs. 2000 (approximately) in addition to insurance for a capital sum of Rs.20,000 per year. Nine such schemes are already in operation. The scheme envisages insurance to 10,000 workers during 1999-2000.
Medical Attendance Scheme	By this scheme, tappers undergoing modern allopathic treatment owing to illness are eligible for reimbursement of the expenses incurred for treatment. The maximum benefit extended to a tapper under the scheme is Rs. 1500 per year and expensive treatment for major diseases like cancer, cardiac problems etc, shall be reimbursed with an additional amount of Rs. 5000 or 25% of the actual expense whichever is less, as one time payment during the applicant's life time. In addition to this, Rs. 500 per tapper is granted for undergoing family planning operation.
Housing Subsidy Scheme (3 Schemes)	This scheme is implemented for assisting tapper for constructing own houses. As per the scheme, a tapper constructing a house having a plinth area of 20 to 70 m^2 by spending an amount not exceeding Rs. 130,000 will be entitled to a subsidy of Rs. 7,500 after reaching lintel level of construction. Three separate schemes are being implemented for tappers in the marginal holding sector (0.75 to 1.25 ha), non-marginal holding sector (above 1.25 ha) and organised sector.
Scheme for Providing Sanitary Facilities	It provides assistance for constructing latrines by tapper in the unorganised sector. The assistance is restricted to 75% of the estimated cost of construction or Rs. 3000 whichever is less.
Housing and Sanitary Subsidy Scheme to SC/ ST Workers in the Unorganised Sector	This scheme implemented with the involvement of the Rubber Producer's Societies is meant for the SC/ST community among tapper, in the unorganised sector. The financial assistance will be limited to 25% of the cost of construction or Rs. 14,000 whichever is less for a tapper who constructs both a house and a latrine.

Source: Rubber Board, 2000.

Emerging Issues

On the whole, the analysis of employment, wages, organisational aspects and legislative and welfare measures bring out some important issues in the context of tappers in small holdings. The tappers are found deprived of adequate earnings from tapping and even skilled and experienced tappers are unable to earn comparable wages *vis-à-vis* their counterparts in general agriculture. The findings indicate that some of the specific issues of the sector deviate considerably from the popular perception and conceptualisation of the rural labour market in Kerala. Firstly, the sector exhibits a strikingly lower average daily wages and a near stagnation in wages for the past few years, which is quite contrary to the widely conceived existence of higher wages in the rural labour markets, which is believed to be thwarting the development prospects of the state. Secondly, while the general labour market is more or less characterised with a paradoxical existence of higher wages alongside acute shortage of labour in select occupations, the shortage of labour is not still an acute issue in rubber tapping, despite a considerable span of depression in wage front. The third and most important deviation is the nearly absence of trade unions in the wage setting process, which is quite unanticipated in a state like Kerala, which is otherwise known as the cradle of Indian trade unionism. Finally, unlike other sectors, which are characterised by strong presence of legislative protection and welfare measures, the tappers in small holdings do not derive much security from such interventions. All these findings, warrants a deeper understanding of the dynamics of employment relations in the sector, which is attempted in Chapter VI.

NOTES

1. According to a recent study the relative share of part-time farmers among the rubber was reported to be of significant proportions across the regions in the state and it was exceptionally high in the southern region (78 per cent) compared with the central region

(52 per cent) and northern Kerala (24 per cent). The share of hired labour for tapping has been the highest in the southern region at 94 per cent, followed by 87 per cent in the central region and 44 per cent in the northern region (George, 1999).

2. In cases where family labour is involved, on an average their contribution included 2-3 man-hours of intensive work. The lower participation of women during the initial hours of tapping is mainly due to their engagement in domestic chores. Preparing breakfast and lunch, sending the younger ones to schools, cattle care and so on are carried out by women members, before their joining of the tapper (along with some food, in most of the cases) as helpers during later hours in the morning (around 8.00-8.30 a.m).
3. To some of the officials of Rubber Board of India, this apprehension was one of the factors that tempted the Board to choose, a logo that illustrates a female tapper at work.
4. Tapping is a highly skilled job and the aspirants have to get trained properly in the job before getting into the work. Normally, the skill of tapping is acquired through apprenticeship or via practicing on other trees with similar bark-width. As improper tapping implies crop loss and permanent damage to the trees, employers are careful in selecting adequately skilled tappers. All these imply entry barrier and higher age of entry to the occupation.
5. Many of the respondents reported that several health problems are associated with the occupation. Back pain and tuberculosis are the most frequently reported diseases.
6. This is not, however, true in the case of Nedumangad, where 45 per cent of the tappers are from OBC, due to the increased share of Muslims.
7. For instance, 23 per cent of the respondents belong to SC/ST communities. The parents or grandparents of all these respondents were engaged in other farm works, including paddy.
8. Since mid seventies, several studies report an acute shortage of farm labour, which led to the conclusion that there is strong non-preference among educated youths of Kerala for 'blue-collar and manually demanding jobs', especially farm work.
9. This point towards the growing caste consciousness among the working class of Kerala. It is a least debated observation that during the recent decades there is a stronger preference among the younger generations of traditionally engaged workers to go out of their socially given occupation and to accept non-labelled occupations such as electrician, plumber and other non-farm occupations. Further, there has not been any evidence to suggest that labour belonging to upper caste is accepting those jobs, which are traditionally reserved for lower castes—for instance paddy labour.

10. As per Rubber Board's estimate the average cropping intensity of rubber is 200 trees per acre (Kurien, 2001).
11. As per the estimates of Rubber Board rain guarding of rubber trees could increase the tapping days by 40-60 days.
12. As discussed in Section 4.4, tapping includes a number of activities ranging from cutting of bark to sheet preparation.
13. This trend has increased during the recent years, due to the ongoing 'rubber crisis' that drastically declined the profitability of the crop.
14. In the estate sector, all sorts of wages, including tapping wages are based on time-rates, which are frequently revised as per the recommendations of Plantation Labour Committee. Moreover, the organised rubber plantations are strictly governed by the provisions of the Plantation Labour Act, 1951, which ensures adequate employment and social security measures.
15. A block, as per the Rubber Board's definition, refers to 300 trees.
16. Piece rate wage is meant not only for tapping, but also for the entire activities, which include apart from tapping, the collection of latex and coagula as well as sheet preparation. To complete all these work in a holding with 300-400 trees, implies about 6-8 hours of continuous work for an adequately skilled and experienced tapper.
17. The table is based on the wages reported by the tappers. There existed some variations in wage rates in multiple plot engagements, and the data pertains to the highest wage received across plots.
18. A recent study (Viswanathan *et al.*, 2003) attributed the higher wages in rubber holdings of Central Kerala (covering the districts of Kottayam, Ernakulam and Idukki districts) to the relative labour shortage in the region as well as to the region's much accredited status of being the pioneering region of rubber plantations, acting as the wage setting/signalling point. However, the major defect of this generic conclusion is that it does not take into account the intra-spatial disparities within the region (especially in terms of size of holdings).
19. The region lies far away from urban centres and falls adjacent to the Palode Reserve Forest Region, and thus alternative employment opportunities are extremely limited.
20. A few workers in the study region had earlier worked in the trade unions of estate sector, such as tapping *thozhilali union* (tapping workers union) and estate workers union. These workers are found continuing some links with their earlier trade unions, and even claimed during the survey that they are the members of these unions. A detailed enquiry revealed that some trade unions in the estate sector (especially those with some political party affiliation) are trying to expand their reach to the holding sector too.

6

Labour Contracts in Small Holdings

The structural changes in the small holding sector of rubber and its impact on employment, earnings, wages, and organisational aspects are suggestive of the uniqueness of the labour market of tappers. The exceptional features of the labour market could be better understood through the analysis of the institutional arrangements—types of contracts and labour recruitment and retaining strategies. With this view, the present chapter focuses on the contractual arrangements in the small holding rubber sector. Being the coordinating institutional structure of the labour markets, contractual arrangements depict, to a greater extent, the dynamics of rural labour markets. Contracts allow individuals to make better use of their specific endowments in imperfect markets and to arrive at combinations of income, effort and risk that reflect on both their endowments and the choice preferences.

Labour Hiring Systems and Contracts

Labour relations in small holding rubber sector of Kerala are primarily based on informal contractual arrangements between growers and tappers, which is distinct from the highly impersonal and institutionalised labour relations[1] in the other sectors of rural Kerala, characterised by the presence of a highly unionised labour force even in informal as well as traditional occupations[2]. In all the study regions, contractual arrangements were found informal and unwritten, which are based on a mutual consensus arrived at orally between the growers and tappers. The entry into or renewal of informal work contracts are normally done at the time of commencement of the tapping season, subsequent to the monsoon months or the period of tapping rest, when both the parties clarifies their terms regarding the details of various contractual parameters, such as system and rate of wage, operations included in tapping, extra wage benefits such as bonus and off-season advance, working hours and so on. If some variables are not specifically discussed, they are understood as 'according to customary practices and social norms'. Formal and written contracts are unheard of in the sector, as both tappers and growers are found treating personal dealings as most desirable.

As all the farm labour contracts, simultaneously provides access to land to a 'landless' labour, it also allows a labourless landlord to acquire the labour. Thus, both the parties would look at the desirability of the contract from their on view-points perceived on the basis of benefits. While the grower would be interested in getting a worker with least cost and commitments, the workers would like to assure a reasonable level of employment, with lesser commitments and greater freedom and flexibility at work and workplace. Thus, in a labour abundant situation, the employer would be positioned favourably, as there is an ample scope for getting enough workers. Here, the employer, who has potential levels of employment to offer, would enjoy greater levels of freedom, and force the worker to accept temporary status, which would free the employer from all long term obligations. However, the above behaviour of employers is constrained by the skill requirements for the job. Even in labour abundant situations, employers may have to resort to long-term contracts, if skill requirement for the occupation is higher and thus may be faced with a shortage of labour. This would be more so, in situations of small holding farming where the quantum of work available is too meagre to provide a reasonable level of employment to the worker. Here, the employer is left with less freedom and would be forced to device attractive terms and longer contractual relations for tying labour.

Contractual Tenure: Permanent *versus* Annual Contracts

The 360 respondents in the survey are found working in 595 plots. The details on contractual arrangements were thus based on the plots wise information provided by the respondents. A considerable proportion of the respondents (65. 7 per cent) report that they are engaged in annual contracts where the contractual commitment is for a particular tapping season, while the rest have reported working with long-term or permanent contracts. This predominance of annual contracts is complete in the case of Nedumangad. Notwithstanding this, Kanjirappally showed a strikingly different pattern in reverse direction, where 95 per cent of the tappers are engaged in permanent contracts (Table 6.1.)

Table 6.1: Distribution of Total Plots as per Tenure of Contracts

Tenure of Contract	*Perumbavoor*	*Kanjirappally*	*Nedumangad*	*Total*
Pemanent/ long term	19 (7.5)	185 (94.9)	—	204 (34.3)
Annual/ Seasonal	233 (92.5)	10 (5.1)	148 (100.0)	391 (65.7)
Total	252 (100.0)	195 (100.0)	148 (100.0)	595 (100.0)

Source: Survey Data.
Note: Figures in parentheses are percentages to respective totals.

An exploration into the unique characterisation of Kanjirappally in terms of preponderance of permanent contracts, reveals that unlike their counterparts in Nedumangad and Perumbavoor, small holding growers in Kanjirappally are found entertaining a more 'professional' approach towards the running of the farms. The growers from this locality showed an increased preference to keep experienced workers on a continuous basis, as the quantum and superiority of produce as well as quality of tapping are directly and strongly related to work experience of the tapper. The possible reasons for this preference for engaging tappers on a long-term basis could be attributed to several factors. Firstly, most of the small growers in Kanjirappally are well versed in best practices of rubber cultivation, as the region has a long history of rubber cultivation. Further, compared to their counterparts in other regions, most of these growers were found primarily occupied in farm work, a status that allow them to identify and retain trust-worthy and more experienced tappers. Thirdly, the average holding size of Kanjirappally (3.17 acre) was found much more larger compared to Nedumangad (2.01 acre) and Perumbavoor (1.15 acre), which *inter alia* provides the farmers some incentive to produce quality rubber sheets, due to the advantages available through economies of scale. Fourthly, as explained in the earlier chapters, Kanjirappally shows a relative shortage of skilled tappers, which has led to the engagement of low skilled migrant labour.

A detailed probing into the nature of these 'permanent contracts', however, reveals that the contracts in Kanjirappally are no way different from that of the other areas. The reporting of 'permanent' status is more or less based on the perception of the workers rather than the legitimacy or social validity of the term. The tappers were found engaged in annual contracts, which are for a tapping season. The contractual commitments are to be renewed after every tapping season, after calculating and settling the accounts between both the parties for the completed season. However, *de facto*, these contracts were treated as permanent, as both the growers and the tappers knew that the same worker would continue for a long term under the existing circumstances. This act of treating permanent contracts as annual and the tappers, 'temporarily permanent' is mainly to insulate growers from the risk of long-term commitments and some of the adverse implications, which are specially contemplated, given the socio-political premise of Kerala. Growers reported that providing formal and permanent status to the tapper would enhance their vulnerability, while settling issues such as payment of compensation, in the event of retrenchment or felling the trees. Further, it is feared that retaining workers for longer period would lead to undesirable disputes and pave way to the entry of trade unions in employer-employee relations. This fear of growers to recognise tappers as permanent workers, often adversely affect the tappers in realising the benefits of certain welfare schemes, which are meant for the small growers. For instance, as discussed in Section 5.7, the Rubber Board provides several benefits to the tappers in small holding sector, who have completed a certain minimum years of service. To apply for these benefits, the tapper has to produce a certification from the grower. In many a cases, the grower denies this certificate to the worker.

Most of the growers believe that formalising the contracts and providing the tappers some permanent status would boomerang, as it happened to the Kerala farmers during the tenancy and land reforms of the 1970s. Here, it is to be noted that the petty bourgeoisie in Kerala agriculture is still not recovered from the shock that they have undergone during the golden age of worker mobilisation and government initiated redistributive regime. Even during an era of footloose situation of the workers, the farmers are taking extra caution to counter any unanticipated adversarial claims from the working class. Thus, it is evident that the imprints left by the trade unions in their golden age and the pro-labour stand of the earlier governments, still have some impact on the behavioural pattern of cultivators, affecting the employment relations in agriculture.

In the other study regions, annual contracts are found prominent with lesser commitment for extending the contracts in the coming seasons. Growers though reported of their interest to retain tappers continuously, are not willing to meet the long-term obligations/commitments towards this. In the absence of an assurance of employment security, the tappers are also found committing their services only for a season/year, as it provided them more freedom and flexibility in future labour market decisions. Even in these regions, mostly tappers are found continuing with the same grower for a long period of time. Table 6.2 gives the distribution of 595 plots across the number of years of engagement of the respondents.

Table 6.2: Distribution of Plots across Number of Years of Engagement of Respondents

Years of engagement	*Perumbavoor*	*Kanjirappally*	*Nedumangad*	*Total*
Upto 2 years	25 (9.9)	5 (2.6)	30 (20.3)	60 (10.1)
2-4 years	53 (21.0)	18 (9.2)	46 (31.1)	117 (19.7)
4-6 years	31 (12.3)	12 (6.2)	49 (33.1)	92 (15.5)
6-8 years	119 (47.2)	41 (21.0)	14 (9.5)	174 (29.2)
8-10 years	20 (7.9)	62 (31.8)	7 (4.7)	89 (15.0)
More than 10 years	4 (1.6)	57 (29.2)	2 (1.4)	63 (10.6)
Total	252 (100.0)	195 (100.0)	148 (100.0)	595 (100.0)

Source: Survey Data.
Note: Figures in parentheses are percentages to respective totals.

Irrespective of the regions it could be seen that tappers continue in the same plots for several years. In 54.8 per cent of the plots the tappers were reported working for more than 6 years. However, some region-wise differences are noticed. In Kanjirappally, the proportion of workers with more than 6 years constituted for more than 80 per cent. The increased preference for long-term contracts is further evident from the fact that 30 per cent of plots have tappers with more than 10 years. In Perumbavoor also, tappers are found sticking to same farms for several years though the proportion of tappers in the category of more than 8 years of engagement was quite lower compared to Kanjirappally. Maximum number of plots in the region (119 out of 252) has retained the same worker for a period of 6-8 years. Quite contrary to this pattern, in Nedumangad comparatively short-term engagement of tappers is more prominent, where only 15 per cent of plots have the same tapper for more than 6 years. In brief, the survey findings indicate the prevalence of long-term contractual associations, though there is a visible resistance by growers in recognising and legalising these arrangements as 'permanent'. Tappers also find long-term dealings more useful, as it results in the reduction of transaction costs especially related to recurring efforts for job search.

Nature of Wage Payments: Piece-rate Wages *versus* Product Share

As discussed in an earlier chapter, piece rate wage payment is found to be the dominant mode of wage payment in the study areas, with 95.56 per cent of respondents primarily working with the arrangement. The rest of the tappers are found working with product sharing arrangements, which is a recent development subsequent to the depression in rubber prices. While the piece rate wages is visibly prominent in Perumbavoor (93 per cent) and Nedumangad (96 per cent) in Kanjirappally, the prevalence of the system is complete. This pattern gives rise a fundamental question related to the contract choice in small holding sector as to why the small holding sector has a strong preference towards piece rate wage payment system, over the arrangements of product sharing or time rate wage payment. It is presumed that both the actors in the labour market (the growers and tappers) are believed to contemplate the advantages and disadvantages of various options, before getting into a particular arrangement. Nevertheless, any existing system of wage payment need not be considered as the optimal one preferred by both of the actors or even either of them. Apart from these preferences, the comparative power relations of the actors also matter while adopting and following particular arrangements in the labour market. The following tables (Table 6.3—6.6) compare the perceived advantages and disadvantages of wage payment contracts against product share arrangements, as well as piece rate system *vis-à-vis*, time rate arrangement.

As summarised in Table 6.3 to the growers, the advantages of wage contract are high when the prices in the product markets are fairly high. However, resorting of wage contracts pause several issues to the grower such as: (a) the burden of wage payment to the worker even without realising the revenue from sale of the produce; (b) increased levels of transaction costs, especially in monitoring the work effort; and (c) the risk of losing a higher share of revenue towards labour cost at times of market crisis.

Table 6.3: Advantages and Disadvantages of Wage Contract and Product Share Arrangement: Growers' Point of View

	Wage Contract	*Product Share*
Advantages	• Higher profitability in times of better prices to the produce.	• Reduced labour cost in times of depressed prices for the produce. • Convenience of deferred payment. • Reduced level of transaction cost to ensure quantum and quality of produce.
Disadvantages	• Inconvenience of immediate payment to labour. • Increased transaction cost to ensure quantum and quality of produce • Lower profitability in times of product market crisis	• Lower profitability in times of product market boom

On the contrary, the farmer, at times of price slash in the market, generally prefers the product share arrangement. As discussed in the earlier chapter, in the study regions following the rubber crisis, which started in the mid 1990s, there is a tendency from the growers to shift towards product sharing arrangements. The other perceived advantages of product sharing arrangement include convenience of deferred payment and the reduced levels of transaction costs, especially in monitoring. The argument that product sharing would reduce transaction costs in terms of monitoring and supervision, however, holds good only when there is a long-term relationship and mutual loyalty between the actors. If the tapper is only attached for a short term, probably, the transaction costs would be higher in product sharing arrangement, as there would be a tendency for the tapper to ruthlessly cut the trees so as to maximise his/her short run earnings.

From the tappers point of view, as summarised in Table 6.4, the wage contracts are more desirable at the time of crisis in the product market. Also, wage contracts provide the worker some degree of clarity regarding their wage income.

Table 6.4: Advantages and Disadvantages of Wage Contracts and Product Share Arrangement: Tappers' Point of View

	Wage Contract	*Product Share*
Advantages	• No risks during price fall in the product market. • Certainty in term of earnings.	• Better share during boom in the product market. • Lesser interference of employer to ensure quantum and quality of produce.
Disadvantages	• Lesser share in profits during price rise in the product market. • Increased interference of employers to ensure quantum and quality of work.	• Risk during price fall in the product market. • Uncertainty in terms of earnings.

The major disadvantages perceived by the workers in the wage contracts is the possibility of deriving a lesser share in profits, at times of product market boom and the increased interference of growers to ensure the enforceability of the contract. Conversely, the tappers would consider product-sharing arrangements as desirable when the price of the produce in the market is fairly high. Also it provides more freedom and flexibility at work, as there would be lesser interference from the growers.

Similar to the above, both the growers and tappers have their own considerations on preferences and dislikes while choosing between piece rate wages and time rate wages. Table 6.5 summarises the perceived advantages and disadvantages of both the systems in the growers' viewpoint. The perceived advantages of piece rate tapping to the grower include: (a) higher incentive for the tapper to work and resultant increase in productivity; (b) reduced incentive for the worker to shirk and resultant reduction in monitoring costs; and (c) more availability of workers due to flexible timing. From the table, it is evident that the advantages and disadvantages of time rate wage contracts are diagonally opposite to that of piece rate contracts.

Table 6.5: Advantages and Disadvantages of Piece Rate and Time Rate Tapping: Growers' Point of View

	Piece rate tapping	*Time rate tapping*
Advantages	• Possibility of increased effort per worker and more output • Reduced possibility of shrinking and resultant reduction in monitoring costs	• Possibility of increased lactation period and increased long runs total returns due to careful tapping. • Higher quality produce.
Disadvantages	• Possibility of reduced lactation period and lower long run returns due to careless tapping. • Risk of Poor quality produce.	• Possibility of reduced effort per worker and less output. • Increased monitoring cost on avoidance of shrinking

From the tappers' view point (Table 6.6), the major advantages of piece rate system of wage payments are: (a) built-in incentives for increasing the effort; (b) more flexibility and higher freedom at work; and (c) the scope of utilising the assistance of family labour. However, the major drawback with the system is that the tapper has the risk of under employment and thus reduced daily earnings which is especially so in the small holding situations. Time rate system, on the other hand, provides employment assurance to the worker. At the same time, it is characterised with less freedom and flexibility and absence of incentive to work. Also, the latter has no incentive for utilising the available family labour.

From the foregoing discussion, it is evident that both the small holders and tappers have a series of concerns while choosing a particular contractual arrangement. And, it is reasonable to believe that the existing contractual set-up to some extent explains the comparative power relations of the actors. The fact that piece rate is the predominant system of wage payment, shows the highly exploitative nature of work contract in the sector. In a piece rate arrangement, as the wage earnings of the tapper is directly related to the quantum of work effort, the tapper finds its imperative to work hard even without minimum levels of leisure.

Table 6.6: Advantages and Disadvantages of Piece Rate and Time Rate Tapping: Tappers' Point of View

	Piece Rate Tapping	*Time Rate Tapping*
Advantages	• Incentive for increasing effort. • More flexibility in working time • Reduced interference of employers through supervision and monitoring • Higher scope for utilising family labour	• Assured employment and earnings • Fixed timing for work and leisure
Disadvantages	• Highly exploitative and effort demanding without much scope for leisure • Risk of underemployment and low earnings, especially in small holdings	• No incentive for increasing effort • Rigidity in working hours • Increased interference of employers through supervision and monitoring • Lower scope for involving family labour

System of Advances or Voluntary Indebtedness

An important feature of the prevailing contractual arrangements in the rubber holdings of Kerala is the interlocking of the tappers and growers through a unique scheme of wage payment, which often assumes the nature of a voluntary system of indebtedness. In all the study regions, the majority of the tappers are found receiving wages in terms of weekly advances, which were popularly referred as *'chelavu kasu'* or *'kaikkasu'* (living expenses). The proportion of tappers who follow the advance system is highest at 93 per cent in Nedumangad, followed by 83 per cent in Perumbavoor and 79 per cent in Kanjirappally. The weekly advances, ranging between Rs. 200 and Rs. 350, are found disbursed on a particular day (Saturday or Sunday in most of the cases). The norms for fixing advance amount include the quantum of work (tapping task), levels of skill and experience of the tapper, years of service of the tapper with the particular employer, and the 'overall reputation' of the tapper in the locality. The details of tapping carried out by the worker are normally noted in the '*tachu book*' (work book) kept with the farmer[3]. The settling of these advance amounts is normally once in a year, at the time of Christmas or Onam. In a few cases this was done on a monthly basis (14 cases in Perumbavoor, 12 in Nedumangad) and in some other cases, on weekly basis (22 in Nedumangad). The reduced interval of settling of the accounts was more prominent with those growers, who could not afford to take the risk of paying a huge arrear amount at the time of annual settlement. Of late, subsequent to the slow down in the natural rubber market, many a farmer are found switching over to a system, where the accounts are found settled only at the time of sale of the rubber sheets. This is especially so with small and tiny holders in Perumbavoor and Nedumangad (17 and 23 cases respectively), who are not able to settle the huge sums of wage dues, unless the crop is sold at the market, at a favourable price.

Usually, at the time of settlement, the worker would be paid the wage arrears, if the tapping wages due to him/her exceeds the '*chelavu kasu*' that s/he had already received and *vice versa*. However, in most of the cases, the accounts were found carried over as the next year's/month's opening balance. In the study regions, this practice of carrying forward the arrears to the next year's account was often found assuming the form of a voluntary system of indebtedness or bondage.

Interlinked Transactions

Interlinked contracts could be defined as transactions in more than one commodity or service made between the same pair of individuals and linked in an essential way. Thus, two contracts are not interlinked if one of the contracts could have taken place independently with no additional cost to either party. Thus, an essential feature of interlinking is that delinking the contracts would be infeasible or costly for at least one party (Braverman and Srinivasan, 1981). In the above sense, though the small holding rubber farms show certain level of interlinked transactions such as extension of credit, provision of perquisites and so on these could be strictly seen as a collusion of land, labour and credit market as discussed in literature related to agriculture in other parts of India. Thus, interlinked transactions in small holding sector of rubber could be seen more as a labour tying mechanism, through which growers retain skilled labour and develop moral ties.

Interlinked transactions through provision of extra contractual support was found as an effective mode to forge long-term relationship between growers and tappers. Even the system of advance wage payment followed in rubber holding could be conceptualised as a form of interlinked transactions. The payment of extra wage benefits such as festival advance, bonuses and other sorts of advances are not formally included in the work contract, though these extra wage benefits are provided differently across regions and as per the individualised understanding between tappers and growers. Table 6.7 gives details of extra contractual support received by the respondents in 595 plots.

Table 6.7: Percentage Distribution of Plots in Terms of Extra Contractual Support

Type of support	*Perumbavoor*	*Kanjirappally*	*Nedumangad*	*Total*
Wage Advances	199 (79.0)	146 (74.9)	137 (92.6)	482 (81.0)
Off season Advances	156 (61.9)	154 (79.0)	53 (35.8)	363 (61.0)
Bonus/Gift during festivals	40 (16.0)	97 (49.7)	15 (7.7)	72 (12.1)
Personal/Consumption Loans	134 (53.2)	76 (39.0)	39 (26.4)	249 (41.8)
Mid-morning Tea/ Breakfast/Snacks	116 (46.0)	74 (37.9)	113 (76.4)	303 (50.9)
Provision of other employment during off-season	58 (23.0)	84 (43.1)	80 (54.1)	222 (37.3)
Support in Socio-political life	146 (57.9)	45 (23.1)	56 (37.8)	247 (41.5)

Source: Survey Data.
Note: Figures in parentheses are percentages to total number of plots.

Provision of credit was reportedly stronger in all the study regions, prior to the period of rubber crisis. The system of interest free consumption loans and off-season advances with long repayment period was more prominent and it was reported that the average debt amount that was being carried over to next season as outstanding loans towards the growers at any point of time would run into few thousands. However, with the crisis, the extent of such credit availability is highlighted to have declined though the system is still prevalent. In all the study regions, financially well-off farmers continue to provide consumption loans/off-season advances and render financial help in times of contingencies. Tiny growers with weak resource base however, find these monetary assistances unfeasible as they cannot afford this and there is a risk of non-repayment by workers. However, to compensate for the absence of monetary assistance tiny growers, are found entertaining friendly relationships with the tappers through extension of non-monetary help during emergencies. Further, in some cases, it is found that in the event of unforeseen incidentals and emergencies, the tappers are found borrowing from the farmers, where the loan amount (either fully or partially) is carried over into the *'thachu book'*. Some of the tappers reported receiving one time annual bonus (at the time of Christmas or *Onam*) and /or off-season advance payments. The system of bonus is more prominent in Kanjirappally. In 32 per cent of plots, tappers reported the existence of bonus, the amount of which ranged between Rs. 300-1500. The grower usually decides the amount arbitrarily. In Perumbavoor 8 workers (in 10 plots) reported of bonus while in Nedumangad the system is completely absent. However, in certain cases a system of giving of new clothes/gifts is found existing in place of bonus system. Off-season payments were found prominent in both Kanjirappally and Perumbavoor where the tappers received some *ad hoc* payments during rainy season, which would be eventually transferred to the *'thachu book'*. The quantum of off-season advances varied from case to case depending upon several considerations such as the experience of the tapper, the perception of growers about the integrity of the worker and so on.

A large proportion of tappers (50.9 per cent) have reported receiving perquisites, such as tea, breakfast and snacks and gift during festivals, even though these are not part of the wage contract. The other extra contractual supports include provision of agriculture work in the holdings during off-seasons and societal and political helps (such as extension of recommendations in times of school/college admission of wards, treatment in hospitals and so on).

Contractual Enforcement and Social Compliance

Despite the informal and unwritten nature of the contracts, there is a mutual and 'implicit' understanding between the growers and tappers to stick on with the contractual obligations. The observance and enforcement of the informal agreements are ensured through societal norms and rules of the community. In small community agrarian economies, dishonest behaviour tends to be detected by the neighbours in the community and conveyed quickly to another party and thus both the actors are discouraged from the breach of trust given the severe cost of a loss of reputation in the event of discovery.

The social norms or rules are understood in a relative manner, where the growers' obligations are defined as per 'those followed generally by other growers in the region' and tapper's duties are conceived at par with those agreed upon and observed by an 'average worker' in the vicinity. Due to the repetitive nature of the contractual dealings, both the parties fear that their non-compliance of contractual terms would adversely affect their future continuance in the field. A grower, who provides lower wages and denies customarily prevailing benefits to the tappers, would find it difficult to get workers in the subsequent seasons/years, due to the social dishonour attached to the non-compliance. Similarly, a tapper who fails to fulfil contractual commitments would eventually find it difficult to ensure employment for the subsequent terms[4].

Thus, there is a mute consensus between both the parties that any breach of trust or deviation from the socially accepted and informally agreed upon contractual terms, would be followed with social sanctions and interventions from extra-contractual actors, including peer group members, trade unionists, political leaders and socially acceptable mediators. Here, the social punitive action attached with violation is slightly distinct from that portrayed by Krishnan (1991), while theorising Kerala's rural labour market as a whole, as the stigma in this case cuts across both the classes—the growers and tappers.

Both the parties consider breaking the contract during the currency of its tenure as 'unethical'. Normally, once the tappers are contracted for a season, they are found to stay on till the work is completed and do not leave in the middle, even when they perceive better remunerative alternatives. In return, the tappers expect the growers also to reciprocate in the same fashion. For instance, some of the respondents while recollecting past years of work, were found vociferously criticising those growers, who retrenched[5] or replaced[6] tappers during the middle of the season. Most of the growers were reported restraining themselves from changing the worker in the currency of a tapping season, to the extent possible. All these are indicative of the moral and emotional sanctity attached by both the actors (growers and tappers) to the mutely specified contractual obligations.

Renewal of Contracts and Contractual Parameters

As mentioned elsewhere, contracts are renewed or broken after every tapping season, where both the actors (both growers and tappers) reconsider and negotiate on the various contractual parameters, such as wages, other monetary benefits and terms of engagement. Generally, prior to the commencement of each season, the tappers among themselves were found informally arriving at a consensus regarding what could be the next years' wage. This consensus is reached through informal discussions among the tappers. Normally, there would be an understanding among the tappers regarding the lowest wage that could be accepted. In other words, tappers collectively but tacitly decide on the lower limits for wages during the season. The parameters which are considered while deciding on the wage and other benefits to be bid for the next season include the ongoing prices of product (rubber) in the market, the relative wages in tapping *vis-à-vis* alternative jobs, the increased cost of living, the profitability of the grower and so on. The tappers also find using the latest available tripartite agreements on wages in related sectors or government notifications on minimum wages as a benchmark in revising the contractual parameters[7].

More or less, the tappers were found strongly honouring and adhering to the decisions, which are collectively taken. However, the degree of commitment to collective decisions is rather weak, compared to the situation of social punitive action described by Krishnan (1991), while explaining the deterrents from the social stigma attached to betraying the peer group decisions, in rural Kerala. During the survey, which was coincided with a crisis period in the rubber sector, many tappers were found working with wages below the collectively agreed upon wages. Here, the wages were found decided as per the one-to-one relations between the tapper and grower, which in most cases are not revealed. This *inter alia* lead to a situation of 'double collusion', where the worker gets into an implicit cooperation agreement, on the one hand with his peers, and entertains a one-to-one collusive formula with the growers, which in most cases deviate from the collective decisions of tappers. As explained in Chapter 5, irrespective of the regions, the wages were found stagnating around the present levels, for the past few years. In view of the crisis, non-revision of wages was understood by most of the tappers as an unavoidable option as the growers are also equally hit by the product market crisis. In some isolated cases, to ensure employment; tappers even expressed their readiness to work at a lower wage than the prevailing wages, in the event of continuing crisis.

This phenomenon of complete absence of resistance towards non-revision of wages for almost 6 years, despite the increases in cost of living and relative wages of alternative rural occupations is quite distinct from the overall labour scenario of the state. Several reasons could be attributed to these unusual labour relations in small holding sector of natural rubber. Firstly, given the fact that employers themselves are small growers, with minimum levels of land, there is not much scope for a class tension or antagonism between exploited and exploiter. Most of the tappers, especially in Nedumangad and Perumbavoor, were found not considering their employers as bourgeoisie. Secondly, tappers were found morally bound to accept wages at the existing levels during crisis in view of the fact that wage rates had been higher than the market clearing wages throughout 1980s till the mid 1990s, when product prices were impressive. The third and most important factor is the near absence of trade unions in the picture, which has led to a situation where the tappers are not in a position to successfully organise any resistance even when wages are low with deteriorating working conditions.

This kind of docility and submissiveness of workers, however, is not anticipated in a state like Kerala, where the workers are otherwise known for militancy and even reported to be involved extreme levels of rent seeking and detrimental practices including extraction of exorbitant wages and charging wages for non-work. This unique profile of labour relations thus warrants a distinct conceptualisation of the contractual relations in the small holding sector of rubber cultivation, which is attempted in the subsequent section.

Rubber Tapping in Small Holdings: An Agency Problem

As discussed in the previous sections, the labour relations in small holding rubber cultivation are distinct from the rest of the rural occupations. The unique relations in this sector could be explained in terms of the processes involved in tapping and the constraints defining the bargaining powers of both growers and tappers, which could be analysed using the framework of agency theory. Tapping in the small holding sector represents a typical agency problem, where the small-grower (principal) is to ensure diligent as well as skilful effort from the tapper (agent). The grower's income from the holdings is directly linked to the quantum and quality of effort from the tappers. The observance of piece rate system could be seen as an effective mechanism to ensure adequate levels of work-efforts without much cost implications. Apart from ensuring quantum of work-effort, in rubber tapping, quality of work also assumes centrality. If the tapper cuts the trees either a little too deeply, or not quite deep enough, the productivity of the trees would be affected. Moreover, improper tapping would lead to permanent loss to the grower through reduced yield and/or damage of trees.

Further, tapping is a regular process, which is carried out throughout the year with a brief period of tapping rest. This brings in the issue of non-observability of tapper's work effort in small holdings. Many of these growers themselves are employed either in farm activities or in other sectors of the economy that they find it impossible to personally supervise the work-effort of the tappers, on a continuous basis, especially due to the odd timing of (early hours of morning, and even before dawn) tapping. Further, diseconomies of small-scale farming make it impossible to introduce paid supervisors, as in the case of the estate sector. The growers are also not in a position to decompose or delineate the exact contribution of the tapper, as the yield is based on several other exogenous factors such as moisture content in the atmosphere, age of the trees, climatic conditions and so on. Thus, the grower cannot exactly attribute a production loss to the tappers laziness or bad work. All these issues cumulatively lead to the problem of non-enforceability of contractual terms. The strong preference for entertaining long-term contract could be seen as an act to counter the issues arising out of non-observability and non-enforceability attached to the rubber tapping.

The growers' concern on enforceability of contractual terms becomes all the more important with the increased prevalence of part-time farming, as in the case of Kerala. To overcome these issues, the growers who find it difficult to monitor the tappers at work throughout the season would be keen to maintain close personal relations with the tappers. Accordingly, there would be a strong preference for devising extra contractual acts of mutual support, which in turn personalise the labour relations so as to check any kind of shirking and moral hazards. The existence of various forms of extra contractual supports, as evident from the earlier discussion thus could be seen as strategy for creating personal or moral ties, which ensures desirable levels of work-effort and cover the moral hazard problems. Developing of close personal relations also allows the small growers to collect sufficient information regarding the tappers' conduct by casual observation and gossiping without undertaking explicit monitoring.

Considerable horizontal ties exist among the workers even when they have entered into contract with different employers. These ties become stronger, if the employers are particularly small holders. This gives rise to unenforceable contracts. In small holding rubber holdings, which are characterised with fragmentation of holdings and multiple employer status of the tappers, the growers are confronted with the issue of horizontal ties among the workers. Here, the interdependence between the principal and agents becomes more complex, and when the network of interdependency widens, the impersonal exchange process gives rise to all kinds of opportunistic behaviour such as cheating, shirking and moral hazards, giving rise to increased levels of transaction costs for the growers. In such circumstances, the nurturing of extra-contractual support systems is found resorted by the growers. As seen earlier, the acceptance of a lower wage below the implicitly and collectively arrived at wages could to some extent explain the strength of personal ties created through provision of extra contractual support.

In the small holding rubber tapping situations, a major constraint faced by the growers is the rigidities in the supply of labour. Tapping needs to be carried out on a regular basis, and the deferring of tapping implies an irreversible loss of output to the grower. Tapping also requires specialised skills and thus the entry is restricted. This leads to a fragmentation of market by skills and tasks. Also, there is stickiness in labour supply in the spatial dimension. Possession of small plots by virtue of land reforms, higher enrolment in schools, relatively smaller gaps in inter-village wage rates and so on are found limiting the scope of mobility of labour from his/her 'locality'. All these constraints, along with incomplete information and difficulties of negotiation and coordination quite often lead to a paradoxical situation of shortage for skilled tappers, in spite of the overall level of unemployment in rural Kerala. This sort of a shortage for labour, often, forces the small farmers to ensure certain inbuilt incentive structures in the contracts. At its minimum level, the grower is to ensure that the tappers are provided with a net pay off which is equal to their reservation income or retention value. In closely interactive rural set-up the ways for doing so are: (a) to provide comparatively higher wages; and (b): to interlink consumption and production credits and other contracts such as insurance (e.g. grower's assistance to tappers' during contingencies). As the former mode is usually practiced during periods of higher prices to rubber and hence higher profitability to the growers, the latter is more or less practiced as a long-term way of tying 'preferred tappers', for longer periods. Through personalisation of relations and interlinking of markets, the growers are found essentially increasing the costs of breach of contractual terms by the tappers. As Becker (1974, 1976) explains in the theory of social interactions, a person will refrain from exercising opportunism to the extent that its expected cost exceeds the expected gain. Accordingly, a tapper may be tempted to exercise opportunism, if the cost of detection is small. In personalised situations with fairly long-term and interlinked contractual prepositions, however, shirking results in the loss of reputation and lucrative future employment opportunities. As discussed earlier, personal relationships are found strengthened through the interlinking of transactions, which often include credit, and social security elements, making the non-compliance of contractual terms costlier to the tapper. Thus, interlinking of transactions helps the growers to ensure loyalty and diligence from the tappers, without following a system of stringent monitoring.

In small holding rubber plantations, compliance of contracts helps both the actors to reduce their respective transaction costs. 'Reputation' gained within the community helps both the growers and tappers in reducing their efforts and resources in repeated interactions. As the social interaction among people are intensive, both the growers and the tappers would be discouraged from behaving dishonestly given the severe loss of reputation in the event of discovery. This leads to a situation where a 'bad worker' finds it difficult to get 'good work' (in quantity and quality), and a 'bad employer' fails to get 'good workers'.

The small rubber holdings further exemplify an agency problem due to the so-called 'adverse selection', especially where the principal is not familiar with the characteristics (e.g. ability) of the agent. The growers are found keen in finding out solutions for this issue, as the farm profits, both short run and long turn, are closely linked to the quality of work and quantum of work effort provided by the tapper. Since there is heterogeneity of labour, the growers preferentially engage workers whom they know to be better workers (Binswanger *et al.*, 1984; Rudra, 1982; Richard and Martin, 1983). In rubber holdings, though there is heterogeneity, inferior tappers (in terms of skill and experience) cannot be paid considerably less than their better counterparts because of the intervention of various factors, including social setting of the labour market. This *inter alia* results in a preference for workers of known ability over those of unknown ability (adverse selection). The growers are found devising several ways to prevent and get rid of adverse selection issues. The lower preference for local tappers, entertaining of long term associations with 'good workers', provision of non-wage benefits and extra contractual support are some of the ways in which the growers are circumventing and addressing such issues. The other implication of this line of reasoning is that it would lead to a situation of excess demand, when the actual supply is adequately sufficient. The perennial shortage of tappers in rubber holdings could be, thus, partially attributed to the preference for better workers by the growers.

The unique set of issues such as non-observability of work-effort, non-enforceability of contractual commitments, non-divisibility of tappers contribution, the heterogeneity of workers (and the resultant adverse selection) and the skilled nature of work (leading to segmentation) makes contractual arrangements in the sector unique compared to other farm occupations. Though the degree of extra wage support and other incentive structures have reported to have reduced considerably during the period of rubber market depression, the tappers find it difficult to negotiate for higher wages or break the contract mainly due to two counts. Firstly, the existence of personal ties for a long period has found to create certain amount of moral binding which deter the tapper to bargain for wage revisions or to resist the withdrawal of existing extra wage benefits. Also, this moral binding prevents the tappers to search for other alternatives in the locality. The personal ties nurtured through incentive structures and the skill rigidity has delimiting the bargaining capacity of the tappers to bid for wage rise or to resist withdrawal of support systems. Secondly, as the revision in piece rate wages is perceived to have strong linkage with the product price, the tappers were found entertaining a hope that the wages would increase at any time if there is any revival in the market price of rubber. The growers were also found convincing the tappers the product market crisis as the rationale for the wage stagnation and the thinning down of other benefits. This could to some extent explain the compassionate attitude entertained by the tappers even when their pay packets are adversely affected. Tappers are found responding to the adverse circumstances, through the adoption of various coping mechanisms, either at the individual level or at the household level. These livelihood strategies are examined in the subsequent chapter.

NOTES

1. Kerala is well known for the organization of labour that cuts across the distinction between 'organised-unorganised' sector and 'formal-informal' sector. This has necessitated institutionalisation of labour relations even in the informal sector (Kannan, 2003).

2. In Kerala, the presence of trade union among rural workers is generally understood as strong and broad based, where the labour attached to general agriculture, toddy tapping, head load work, sand mining, coir making, cashew processing, beedi making, lime shell work and so on are highly organised under trade unions.
3. In some cases, even the walls of thatched sheds or farmhouses were also found substituting *tachu* books, as the farmers/tappers used to scribble their accounts on it.
4. In the framework of infinitely repeated game, which discusses the achievement of a cooperative outcome in a repeated non-cooperative game this situation of mutual compliance is explained as equilibrium attained under the threat of "trigger strategy", where each actor is inviting others to behave 'well' (Osmani, 1991).
5. The retrenchment generally happens, when the grower decides to sell the garden or fell the trees to meet some unexpected financial requirements.
6. Replacement generally happens when the employers find fault with the workers or detects shirking.
7. In game theory, this collusion of workers could be explained as a case of 'implicit-cooperation' or 'tacit collective bargaining' (Osmani, 1991).

7

Livelihood Diversification of Tapper Households

From the analysis in the previous chapters, it is evident that rubber tappers in small holding sector of Kerala, are confronted with a highly exploitative labour relations characterised by piece rate wage system, low wages, poor extra wage support, absence of welfare and social security measures. Though these exploitative conditions existed even during periods of increasing wages, the situation has worsened during a period of falling rubber prices with the erosion of extra wage supports. The near stagnation of piece rate wages during a period of increasing cost of living coupled with the dooming prospects of employment in tapping are found to have affected the livelihoods of tappers. The coping mechanisms of tappers in times of the crisis warrant analysis as it could provide useful insights into the livelihood strategies of rural workers during shocks or adversities, which is attempted subsequently.

Situating the Rubber Crisis

As mentioned in earlier chapters the rubber economy of Kerala in general, and its small holding sector has been undergoing a phase of crisis since 1996 with a trend of price crash of unprecedented scales and proportions. From its all time peak of Rs. 52.04 per kg in 1995-96 the market price of rubber has gone down to Rs. 30.36 by 2000-2001. This drastic decline in rubber prices is widely attributed to faulty import policy and liberalisation of the rubber economy in a globalisation regime that commenced since early 1990s and acquired momentum by the mid 1990s[1].

The integration of Indian market with the world natural rubber price movements since the 1990s is reported to have led to building up of huge surplus stocks. This in turn brought down prices[2], thereby intensifying the problems of growers and implying jeopardy of job prospects to thousands of tappers. Production and supply of natural rubber, far in excess of the domestic needs, has led to a fall in market price of natural rubber (Table 7.1).

Table 7.1: Average Market Price of Rubber in Kerala, 1992-93 to 2001-2002

Year	Price of Rubber (Rs./quintal)
1992-93	2550
1993-94	2569
1994-95	3638
1995-96	5204
1996-97	4901
1997-98	3580
1998-99	2994
1999-00	3099
2000-01	3036
2001-02	3228

Source: Economic Survey, 2002, Government of Kerala.
Note: Prices are for RSS 4 category of rubber.

This unprecedented fall in price of the produce, has affected the profitability of small growers in general. Sales of semi-dried and ungraded sheets, sale of latex and so on have reported to have increased in the recent past, indicating the footloose nature of the growers themselves. To minimise cost of production, wage cuts and deferments in wages or other monetary benefits are being resorted. Several growers have also cut down farm maintenance costs by way of minimising expenses on fertilizer use, pesticide spraying, soil development, land upgradation and even deferring replanting. To minimise the labour costs, a few farmers were also found increasing the frequency of tapping from D/2 to D/3 pattern[3].

All the above developments have adversely affected the prospects and welfare of tappers in small holdings. In many cases, wage payments are deferred till the sale of the produce. It is beyond argument that the penetration of globalisation and the resultant price crisis has led to stagnation in wages, withdrawal of extra wage benefits and adverse employment prospects. The tappers owing to their weak bargaining power, however, did not effectively resist these transformations. This passive behaviour of tappers could be viewed as an outcome of the personally and socially embedded labour relations in the sector and the near absence of trade unions. Given the context of the general crisis in the economy, the tappers are not finding any other alternative employment and are forced to continue with their present engagement[4], despite the fact that the wages are not revised for the past 6 years.

In the event of the adverse conditions of employment and low wages, the workers are found devising various strategies to adapt to the reduction in income. Livelihood adaptation has been defined as continuous processes of changes to livelihoods, which either enhances the existing security and wealth or try to reduce vulnerability and poverty (Davies and Hossain, 1997). In the subsequent section, an attempt is made to capture the livelihood strategies and coping mechanisms of tappers and tapper households during the crisis period. In the analysis tapper household is taken as the unit of empirical investigation, understanding the centrality of the household in designing and constructing strategies as joint responses to an involuntary crisis.

Livelihood Diversification as a Survival Strategy

A livelihood encompasses income, both cash and in kind as well as the social institutions (kin, family, community, village and so on), gender relations and property rights required to support and to sustain a given standard of living. Livelihood strategies are dynamic; they respond to changing pressures and opportunities and adapt accordingly (Ellis, 1998). In the literature on rural livelihoods, livelihood diversification is an important survival strategy of labour households. Livelihood diversification could be seen as a process by which rural families construct a diverse portfolio of activities and social support capabilities in their struggle for survival in situations of livelihood distress. Diversification may occur both as a deliberate household strategy and as an involuntary response to crisis. This acts as a safety valve for rural poor. Diversification is an infinitely heterogeneous social and economic process obeying a myriad of pressures and possibilities in the rural economy. It is differentiated in its causes and effects by location, demography, vulnerability, income levels, education and many other factors. Some main determinants of diversification are seasonality, differentiated labour markets, risk strategies, coping behaviour, credit market imperfections and inter-temporal savings and investment strategies (Ellis, 1998; 2000).

The most important method of livelihood diversification is income diversification. Different individuals and families are likely to possess different income sources. The primary categories of income sources are farm, off-farm and non-farm sources. Farm income includes livestock as well as crop income and comprises both consumption in kind of own farm output and cash income from output sold. Off-farm income typically refers to wage or exchange labour on other farms (within agriculture). It also includes labour payments in kind, such as the harvest share systems and other non-wage labour contracts. Non-farm income refers to non-agriculture income sources. Several secondary categories of non-farm income are commonly identified. These are non-farm rural wage employment, non-farm rural self-employment, property incomes (rent), urban to rural remittances, and international remittances (Saith, 1992).

The subsequent sections analyse the income diversification strategies of tapper households as a survival mechanism during periods of stagnating wages and increased cost of living. In the analysis, the asset status of poor individuals or households is seen fundamental to the understanding of options open to them and adopting survival strategies. Assets include those owned, controlled, claimed, or in some other means accessed by the households. These are basic building blocks upon which households are able to undertake production, engage in labour markets and participate in reciprocal exchanges with other households. The five broad components of assets as identified in the literature are, natural capital (land, water and biological resources), physical capital (buildings, roads, irrigation canals, machines and tools), human capital (family labour, its education, skill and health), financial capital (stocks of money—savings and access to credit) and social capital (social and community relationships and ties) (Carney, 1998; Scoones, 1998; Ellis 2000). In view of the centrality of households as the unit of survival and their assets as the supporting resource base, the household particulars of tappers is provided as a background to the discussion.

Household Characteristics of Tappers

One of the most important assets, possessed by rural labour households is the labour available with the household and hence human capital is a central variable in the livelihood diversification of rural families. The 360 household covered in the study has a total of 1492 members of which 52 per cent are males (Table 7.2). The average family size was found 4.1 for all the regions. Around 65 per cent of the members belonged to the productive working age group (20-60). All regions showed more or less similar patterns in terms of sex composition, family size and working age group. The lower size of the family indicates a limitation in terms of quantum of human capital at the disposal of the household. The prominence of nuclear family pattern suggests that the number of additional hands to support the main income earner is limited to 1 or 2 persons in most of the cases.

Human capital is found increased by education; training and skill development. This determines the labour market prospects of individual members. The education-wise distribution of household members shows that more than 70 per cent of the members are without much educational attainments (below secondary). This in turn is indicative of a constraint in the labour market diversification prospects of tapper families. In the absence of higher qualifications and

Table 7.2: Profile of Tapper Households

	Perumbavoor	*Kanjirappally*	*Nedumangad*	*Total*
Sex				
Male	261 (54.2)	249(50.5)	278(53.8)	788(52.8)
Female	221 (45.9)	244(49.5)	239(46.2)	704(47.2)
Total	482 (100.0)	493 (100.0)	517 (100.0)	1492(100.0)
Age				
Upto 15	79 (16.4)	138 (28.0)	109 (21.1)	326 (21.9)
15-20	49 (10.2)	45 (9.1)	48 (9.3)	142 (9.5)
21-30	111 (23.0)	101 (20.5)	129 (25.0)	341 (22.9)
31-40	74 (15.4)	98 (19.9)	88 (17.0)	260 (17.4)
41-50	75 (15.6)	79 (16.0)	75 (14.5)	229 (15.4)
51-60	56 (11.6)	25 (5.1)	47 (9.1)	128 (8.6)
60 and above	38 (7.9)	7 (1.4)	21 (4.1)	66 (4.4)
Total	482 (100.0)	493 (100.0)	517 (100.0)	1492(100.0)
Education				
No formal Schooling	20 (4.2)	6 (1.2)	30 (5.8)	56 (3.8)
Upto Secondary	308(63.9)	369 (74.9)	387(74.9)	1064(71.3)
Secondary	80(16.6)	56(11.4)	58(11.1)	194(13.0)
Pre-Degree	58 (12.0)	41 (8.3)	37 (7.2)	136 (9.1)
Graduation and above	16 (3.3)	21 (4.3)	5 (1.0)	42 (2.8)
Total	482 (100.0)	493 (100.0)	517 (100.0)	1492(100.0)
Size of Family				
1 member	—	—	1 (0.8)	1 (0.3)
2 members	7 (5.8)	5 (4.1)	3 (2.5)	15 (4.2)
3 members	24 (20.0)	17 (14.1)	8 (6.7)	49(13.6)
4 members	55 (45.8)	67 (55.8)	64 (53.3)	186 (51.7)
5 members	28 (23.3)	26 (21.7)	35 (29.2)	89 (24.7)
6 and above	6 (5.0)	5 (4.2)	9 (7.5)	20 (5.6)
Total	120 (100.0)	120 (100.0)	120 (100.0)	360 (100.0)

Source: Survey Data.
Note: Figures in parentheses are percentages to respective totals.

skills, the opportunities available for diversification of income thus would be limited to those rural occupations, which do not require much formal training or educational attainments. Further, the low human capital base would also constraint the members to access occupations available in the urban localities.

The other important determinant of income diversification for rural households is the natural capital such as land and livestock. As is true of most of the rural households in the state, a large proportion of tapper households (96 per cent) had some land, which was found contributing to the livelihood diversification prospects (Table 7.3).

Table 7.3: Distribution of Tapper Households as per Land Ownership

Status of Land Ownership	*Perumbavoor*	*Kanjirappally*	*Nedumangad*	*Total*
Without Land	6(5.0)	5(4.2)	5(4.2)	16(4.4)
With Land	114(95.0)	115(95.8)	115(95.8)	344(95.6)
Total	120(100)	120(100)	120(100)	360(100)

Source: Survey Data.
Note: Figures in parentheses are percentages to respective totals.

The possession of a dwelling provides security to households to cope with distress situations and to invest on other natural capital, such as cattle and poultry. However, the prospects for diversification would be higher if land is under cultivation. An examination of the distribution of tapper households in terms of possession of cultivated land shows that more than half of the tapper families (54 per cent) have some land under cultivation. Thus, a major source of income diversification in the study regions was the household homesteads, where different crops are cultivated.

Table 7.4: Distribution of Tapper Households as per Land Cultivated

Cultivated Land (in cents)	*Perumbavoor*	*Kanjirappally*	*Nedumangad*	*Total*
1-10	18 (26.1)	4 (14.8)	46 (46.5)	68 (34.9)
11-20	8 (11.6)	5 (18.5)	24 (24.2)	37 (19.0)
21-30	23 (33.3)	1 (3.7)	11 (11.1)	35 (18.0)
31-50	11 (15.9)	4 (14.8)	11 (11.1)	26 (13.3)
51-100	7 (10.1)	10 (37.0)	6 (6.1)	23 (11.8)
Above 100	2 (2.9)	3 (11.1)	1 (1.0)	6 (3.1)
Total	69 (100.0)	27 (100.0)	99 (100.0)	195 (100.0)

Source: Survey Data.
Note: Figures in parentheses are percentages to respective totals.

The region-wise pattern shows variations, where Nedumangad has a higher proportion of households depending on farm work (82.5 per cent). In Kanjirappally however, the proportion was at a lower level of 22.5 per cent. Though the possession of cultivated land was high among the households, from the size-wise distribution, it is evident that more than 70 per cent of these households are with less than 30 cents of land. Thus, a serious limitation is found to exist in terms of the potential of farm work to contribute towards the income diversification of the families. A considerable proportion (37 per cent) of the cultivated plots were with rubber as the main crop (Table 7.5).

Table 7.5: Distribution of Tapper Households as Per Land Under Rubber Cultivation

Cultivated Land (in cents)	Perumbavoor	Kanjirappally	Nedumangad	Total
1-10	—	1 (5.6)	2 (9.5)	3 (4.2)
11-20	8 (24.2)	2 (11.1)	5 (23.8)	15 (20.8)
21-30	14 (42.4)	1 (5.6)	6 (28.6)	21 (29.2)
31-50	4 (12.1)	2 (11.1)	4 (19.1)	10 (13.9)
51-100	6 (18.2)	10 (61.1)	3 (14.3)	19 (26.4)
Above 100	1 (3.0)	2 (11.1)	1 (4.8)	4 (5.6)
Total	33 (100.0)	18 (100.0)	21 (100.0)	72 (100.0)

Source: Survey Data.
Note: Figures in parentheses are percentages to respective totals.

The proportion was 67 per cent in Kanjirappally, 48 per cent in Perumbavoor and 21 per cent in Nedumangad indicating the varying degrees of dependence on rubber as a source of supplementary income to family in these regions. Apart from cultivation of land, the households have reported rearing of cattle and poultry. Around 20 per cent reported of rearing cattle (cow, goat, or pig) While in Perumbavoor and Nedumangad about one-fourth of the households reported dairy farming, in Kanjirappally, the proportion was only around 10 per cent. The scarcity of grazing lands, especially due to the prominence of rubber cultivation in the region was reported as the major reason for this low prominence of cattle. More than 85 per cent of the households reported keeping poultry. This pattern was more or less similar across regions.

Apart from the above-discussed human and natural assets, no other prominent resource supports were reported. As discussed in the earlier chapter, there has been a visible decline in the social capital with the erosion of extra-wage support available to the tappers from the growers in recent years. The extent of social capital available is further constrained by the low resource endowment with other rural labour households. On the whole, the asset status of the tapper households reveals that the possible options for income diversification are limited to three major sources such as farm work, off-farm work and non-farm work.

Farm income includes income arising from farm work by the members of the household, which includes cultivation as well as livestock. Off-farm income refers to wage income arising out of agriculture wage work including tapping by the family members. It also includes payments in kind, such as share of the produce. Non-farm income refers to income from non-agricultural sources such as non-farm rural wage employment, non-farm rural self-employment, property incomes (rent) and remittances.

Subsidiary Sources of Income and Survival Strategies

Conscious reductions in the consumption expenditure of the households or an increased dependence on borrowing (from friends and relatives) were reported as the initial responses to the shrinking of real earnings by most of the respondents. However, in the context of the continuance of the crisis, these adjustments were found unsustainable, which prompted many tappers to resort to diversify the income base of the households. Income diversification strategies of tapper households could be understood at two levels. First is the response of the tappers themselves to a situation of crisis, and the second, the coping mechanisms at the household level.

Responses of Tappers

Due the peculiarity of the process and seasonality involved in rubber tapping, tappers are normally engaged in a number of income augmenting activities, both in the off-season and along side regular tapping job. With the fall in real wages, there is a likelihood that tappers would rely on supplementary income generating activities more than before, either by intensifying or expanding their engagement in subsidiary activities. Corroborating this, the respondents were found engaged a number of activities, the extent of which was reported higher compared to earlier days.

The profile of subsidiary occupation of the workers (Table 7.6) shows that about 60 per cent were engaged in some subsidiary income augmenting activity, which included mostly other agricultural work (47.4 per cent), followed by non-farm engagements including self-employment (35.2 per cent) and farm work in own homesteads (17.4 per cent). Work in the rubber holdings itself was reported to be one of the prominent sources of employment to the tappers. This includes rain guarding of rubber trees, fertilizer application, seedling/clone preparation and other scattered operations. The other major forms of farm sector employment included casual and unskilled works such as land preparation, weeding, manuring and pesticide application.

Table 7.6: Distribution of the Respondents as Per Subsidiary Occupation

Subsidiary Occupation	*Perumbavoor*	*Kanjirappally*	*Nedumangad*	*Total*
Farm Work (Own land)	15 (15.8)	11 (20.4)	11 (17.2)	37 (17.4)
Off-farm Work	46 (48.4)	16(29.6)	39 (60.9)	101 (47.4)
Non-farm work including self employed	34 (35.8)	27 (50.0)	14 (21.9)	75 (35.2)
Total	95(100.0)	54 (100.0)	64(100.0)	213 (100.0)

Source: Survey Data.

Note: Figures in parentheses are percentages to respective totals.

In Perumbavoor and Nedumangad, existence of other agricultural operations including paddy farming in the locality was found to be providing some supplementary income generating opportunities to the workers, especially in post-harvest operations and transportation. Some of the respondents were also found leasing in land for cultivation of crops such as plantain, pineapple and tapioca. Accordingly, off-farm wage work occupied prominence with 60.9 per cent in Nedumangad and 48.4 per cent in Perumbavoor. However, due to the regular nature of tapping, the engagement of tappers in timely as well as skilled operations such as land preparation, transplanting, weeding, manuring and harvesting were almost absent. In Kanjirappally, all the workers who reported subsidiary occupation in the farm sector were found solely engaged in the rubber sector itself, thereby indicating that a large proportion of the tappers in the region are fully relying on rubber holdings for their livelihood.

Non-farm employment is found prominent in Kanjirappally (50 per cent) and Perumbavoor (35.8 per cent) as a subsidiary occupation, which could be attributed to the prominence of the regions as trading centres. The prominent and categories of non-farm wage work include manual work in construction sites, casual works such as transportation, loading and unloading; assistance in shops and establishments and so on. A few tappers were found working as night watchmen, part-time sweepers, lottery ticket sellers, and as collection agents (for chit funds and hire purchase schemes).

Apart from wage employment, self-employment was also found important in these regions. Non-farm self-employment opportunities included petty shops (general provisions, cigarette and so on), repairing centres (cycle and tyre repairing), street vending during evenings, traditional artisanal works (such as blacksmith, cobbler and mat weaving), and allied activities in agriculture (such as dairy farming, fishing and firewood collection). A close analysis of this non-farm employment opportunities point towards several built-in flexibilities attached to these supplementary engagements. Firstly, all these occupations are more or less without any stringent time or with a timing that does not conflict with the time requirement in the rubber holdings. For instance, the engagement in repairing shops in the afternoon and evening street vending are found absolutely suited with the tapping work, as it is done during the early hours of the day. Secondly, many of these self-employment activities are run with complementary involvement of other family members. To suit this requirement, many of the self-employment establishments (such as petty shops or workshops) are found functioning within or very near to the tappers' households. A third way resorted by tappers to supplement the income is to carry out tapping work alongside with their involvement with the other family members or relatives in the traditional jobs such as blacksmithing, carpentry, mat weaving and so on. Though the prominence of farm work in own land was found comparatively lower in all the regions, it was found acting as a shock absorber in many cases. In several cases, the tappers were found utilising their afternoon time in attending the home gardens, and in rearing milch animals. The livelihood diversification process of tappers is further elaborated subsequently through select case studies.

CASE 7.1 : PLANTAIN CULTIVATION IN PANGODE

A tapper of 46 years of age in Pangode Panchayat in Nedumangad has been engaged in tapping work for the past 20 years. He has a 4-member family and owns 60 cents of land of which around 50 cents come under wetland. The wetland was used earlier for cultivating single crop paddy. He works in 2 tiny plots with a total tapping task of about 320 trees in D/1 pattern. The piece rate wage that he receives is 20 paise per tree. The wage was last revised in 1995 from 18 paise. Since then there has been no increase in the wages. In recent years, the tapper finds a considerable increase in living expenses. The situation got worsened when his son has got enrolled in a college in the nearby city for higher education. In view of the gloomy situation prevailing in the rubber sector, he found it difficult to meet the day-to-day expenses of the family. Since he has been working as tapper for so many years he finds it difficult to switch over to some alternative occupations, due to the lack of skills. This prompted him to convert his wet land for plantain cultivation. From 1999 onwards he has been spending his post-tapping hours in the farm and he earns an additional income of about Rs. 4000 per year, which he finds as a relief to cope up with the situation.

CASE 7.2 : MANURING AND SPRAYING OF PESTICIDES

In Vengola Panchayat of Perumbavoor a tapper (39 years) is found engaged in manuring and spraying of pesticides in paddy fields during post-tapping hours, whenever the work is available. He has been working in tapping for the last 14 years and has a family of 6 members. His wife also works as a casual labour in construction work. For around past 4 years he has been working in three tiny holdings, with a total tapping task of about 700 trees. From two plots he receives a piece rate wage of 28 paise and in the third one it is 30 paise. As a consequence of the price crisis about 2 years ago, one of the growers has shifted the plot to D/3 system from the earlier system of D/2. The shifting of tapping pattern reduced his tapping tasks by around 50 trees a day. This combined with the absence of any wage hike for several years forced him to combine some additional work along with tapping. Since he knew pesticides spraying and manuring work in paddy fields he has started accepting these works. Though this work is available occasionally, the high wage rates, especially in the case of pesticide application, helps him to fetch about Rs. 5000 per year.

CASE 7.3 : PINEAPPLE CULTIVATION IN MAZHUVANNOOR

In Mazhuvanoor Panchayat of Perumbavoor a tapper (32 years, working for 13 years) is found cultivating pineapple in leased land to cope up with the stagnating wages in tapping. The tapper is engaged in two plots with a total tapping task of 450 under D/2 tapping. The piece rate wage that the tapper receives is 30 paise. Even before the crisis in rubber sector, the tapper used to combine several activities with tapping due to the low tapping task. The tapper has been clubbing pineapple cultivation along with tapping for the past 4 years. He has started the leasing in for pineapple cultivation in 30 cents of land. After finding its profitability, recently he has taken another plot of 40 cents. In both the plots the tapper has taken the land on product sharing basis (50 : 50). The additional income from pineapple cultivation is about Rs. 4000 per year and he finds it easy to combine both tapping and pineapple cultivation.

CASE 7.4 : OPENING OF CYCLE REPAIR SHOP

In Mundakkayam Panchayat of Kanjirappally, a tapper (30 years, working for the last 8 years) has recently started a cycle repair shop. The tapper is working in a plot with about 900 trees under D/2 pattern where he attends two blocks of trees (300 each). The piece rate wage prevailing at present is 32 paise per tree. Though the wages have been stagnant for past few years, the tapper did not find much problem in meeting the expenses till 2 years before. However, with rising living expenses especially those related to the schooling of children coupled with low wages the tapper has to look for other supplementary sources of income. Due to this, with the help of a bank loan, the tapper has opened a small cycle repair shop. After completing the work in the rubber holdings, around noon the tapper opens the shop and spends his time till late evening. From this the tapper makes, on an average, Rs. 15-25 per day, which helps him to manage the household expenses.

Responses of Households

The other members of tapper households also supplement to the diversification process either by intensifying their involvement in existing engagements or taking up new income generating activities. An important way of augmenting household income is through provision of support to tappers at workplace. The support of the family members in collection and transportation of latex and coagula is found enabling the tapper to enhance the earnings either by increasing the number of trees that could be tapped on a day or facilitating the tapper's engagement in supplementary activities (by releasing the tapper soon after the cutting of trees).

In 68.4 per cent of these cases (119 out of 174), the tappers were found received more than one-hour assistance per day from their family members, which helped them to attend more than 500 trees a day, leading to higher levels of daily wage earnings. This was found especially so in the case of tappers who reported no subsidiary employment. In Perumbavoor, out of the tappers who reported no subsidiary occupation, 88 per cent were assisted by family labour. In Kanjirappally and Nedumangad, the proportions were 67.7 per cent and 60.7 per cent respectively.

Analysis of the occupational profile of other members in tapper households reveals interesting aspects of family's survival. On the whole, 30 per cent (342 out of 1132) of the other members were found engaged in either full time or part time income generating activities (Table 7.7).

Table 7.7: Occupational Distribution of Other Working Members in Tapper Households

Category	*Perumbavoor*	*Kanjirappally*	*Nedumangad*	*Total*
Farm Work (Own land)	26 (24.8)	3 (3.1)	73 (52.5)	102 (29.8)
Off farm Work				
1. Tapping and other works in rubber holdings	23 (21.9)	31 (31.6)	14 (10.1)	68 (19.9)
2. Other Agricultural Work	12 (11.4)	12 (12.2)	42 (30.2)	66 (19.3)
Non-farm work including self employed	44 (41.9)	52 (53.1)	10 (7.2)	106 (31.0)
Total	105 (100.0)	98 (100.0)	139 (100.0)	342 (100.0)

Source: Survey Data.
Note: Figures in parentheses are percentages to respective totals.

Region-wise, this proportion was 29 per cent for Perumbavoor; 26 per cent, for Kanjirappally; and 35 per cent for Nedumangad. In most of these cases of supplementary earning members (84.7 per cent), the tappers were found working with inadequate or lower levels of tapping task (less than 400 trees). Hence, the lower levels of tapping task available to the tappers is found leading to a situation where the worker households are found supplementing to the family income through the entry of an additional member into some income generating activities.

Of the various sources of such activities, off-farm work constituted for the largest share with 39 per cent, followed by non-farm work (31 per cent) and own farm work (30 per cent). However, the pattern showed visible region-wise variations. In Kanjirappally and Nedumangad, non-farm activities accounted for the largest shares with 53 per cent and 42 per cent respectively. In all the regions off-farm work accounted for substantial shares. While in Kanjirappally and Perumbavoor work in rubber holdings (including tapping) assumed importance in off-farm work (31.6 per cent and 21.9 per cent respectively), in Nedumangad, other agricultural work was prominent (30.2 per cent). Considerable levels of variation were visible in terms of the dependency on own-farm work. While more than 50 per cent of family members in Nedumangad supplemented their family income through working in homesteads or rearing livestock in the other regions the share of this category was low (24.8 per cent in Perumbavoor and 3.1 per cent in Kanjirappally). In the subsequent section, through select case studies the livelihood diversification processes of various households are further explained.

CASE 7.5 : FAMILY HELP IN LATEX COLLECTION AND SHEET PREPARATION

In Parathode Panchayat in Kanjirappally, a housewife in a tapper household is helping her husband in latex collection and sheet preparation. The tapper is attending one plot with 650 trees in D/2 pattern (2 blocks). As the earnings from tapping were not sufficient to meet the 5-member family expenses, the tapper has been looking for income supplementing options. About one year back the tapper got a job in a nearby flour mill, where he has to reach by 11.00 a.m. It is not possible for him to finish all the tapping processes till sheet preparation and report for the millwork. In this context, his wife has joined him in tapping. After sending the children to school she reaches the farm at about 9.00 a.m and releases her husband, who must have completed the cutting of trees by then. Subsequently, she collects the latex and prepares the sheets and return home around 1.00 p.m. Through this arrangement, their monthly income has gone up by Rs. 600, which helps them to meet both ends.

CASE 7.6 : DIVERSIFICATION THROUGH CATTLE REARING

In Rayamangalam Panchayat of Perumbavoor, other members of a tapper household have come up with an additional income source to support the collapsing household economy. Though the tapper has tried several options including opening of a vending shop (cigarettes, pan etc.) in the nearby locality, none of these efforts could help the family. In this stage, with the aid of a bank loan, the tapper bought a cow around three years before. At present they have 2 cows and a calf. The members of the family jointly attend the work related to the rearing these cattle. Apart from the earning from tapping, the family makes an additional income of about Rs. 25-30 per day.

CASE 7.7 : HOUSEHOLD MEMBER ENTERING INTO TAPPING

In Koottikkal Panchayat of Kanjirappally, a tapper (50 years) has been working for about 20 years. Currently, the tapper is engaged in two plots with 2 blocks (300 each) of trees in D/2 tapping pattern with a piece rate wage of 32 paise per tree. The continuing depression in the rubber sector coupled with the growing family requirements forced the family members to search for supplementary income sources. Tapper has a family of 5 members, including his wife, son and two daughters. The son who is 23 years has studied up to secondary level and has been looking for some non-farm work such as shop assistants in the nearby Mundakayam town. As he could not find any such job he finally decided to extend support to the family income by undertaking tapping in which he was already skilled. Since, the area has some shortage for skilled tappers it was not very difficult for him to find employment. For the last six months he has been working in a plot of 800 trees with D/2 tapping pattern at 30 paise per tree.

CASE 7.8 : ENTRY INTO MAT WEAVING

In Peringamala Panchayat of Nedumangadu, a tappers' daughter, is found engaged in mat weaving since past 3 years. The tapper (49 years) works in a small plot of 200 trees under D/1 tapping and hence his wage earnings (20 paise per tree) is found too meagre to meet the 4 member family expenses. The financial situation of the family has been crunching with growing debts. At this juncture, his daughter (22 years) joined a skill development programme organised by a cooperative society and learned mat weaving. Subsequently, for the past one and a half years, she has been earning on an average Rs. 500-600 per month, which adds to the family income.

On the whole, it is evident from the foregoing discussion that different livelihood strategies were resorted both by tappers and other household members to maintain the family income during situations of financial shocks. These diversification efforts explain as to how labour households react, readjust and sustain during a period of decline in product prices and subsequent transformations in the labour market.

APPENDIX 7.1

A BRIEF NOTE ON THE CRISIS IN THE NATURAL RUBBER SECTOR

The natural rubber economy of India has witnessed considerable setbacks in the later half of 1990s, due to unprecedented levels of price crash in the product market, which commenced in November 1996. This dwindling fortune in the rubber sector is considered to be the outcome of the inevitable market integration of Indian rubber sector to the international market. Several influential factors are considered to have affected the rubber crisis in India. Firstly, the economic crisis in the South Asian countries during the later half of 1990s and the resultant devaluation of local currencies in Thailand, Indonesia and Malaysia (the three major NR exporters) had serious adverse bearing on the international price of natural rubber.

Further, with the collapse of Third International Natural Rubber Agreement (INRA III), which is again an aftermath of the Asian economic turmoil, the international rubber market was left with no mechanism for price stabilisation. In the domestic market stabilisation also, there was a major policy shifts with the phasing out Buffer Stock Scheme in 1994, which has been an effective system for stabilising the domestic market, introduced at the behest of the Government of India since 1986. Thereafter, the government's control on the price of natural rubber was confined to fixation of benchmark price on the basis of the cost of production of crop as estimated by the Cost Accounts Branch under the Ministry of Finance. As this benchmark price is only a reference price and its notification was not supplemented with any regular measure to ensure its realisation by the growers, it could not make any impact in the market.

The most important factor, which had influenced the natural prices of rubber in India during the 1990s, is the slow down in the international demand growth of natural rubber since the second half of 1996-97 and the resultant accumulation of surplus. The excess supply situation affected the prices of natural rubber in India towards the end of 1996 and the price fall was steep till the end of next year. Though the Government of India intervened in the market by procuring the surplus and brought in some revival in the demand by 2000, the extent of resilience was not strong enough to absorb the entire surplus that have been accumulated during the previous years.

Yet another major factor that has brought in chaos in the domestic market is the problems related to the notification of minimum price as per the provisions of Rubber Act, 1947. It has been pointed out widely that the norms followed in the notification process has made the transactions of RSS 4 and RSS 5 categories of rubber below the minimum price illegal. In absence of any mechanism to intervene in the market, the period immediately after the notification witnessed several problems, the net result of which was the producers being taken to test by the traders as well as consumers. In the nutshell, despite various levels of state intervention in the domestic market, in the form of procurement of surplus and notification of minimum price the objective of realising a sustained recovery was not achieved.

APPENDIX 7.2

GROWERS' RESPONSES TO THE RUBBER MARKET CRISIS AND ITS LABOUR MARKET IMPLICATIONS

The crisis that circumvented the rubber economy of Kerala, following the price slash in the product market since 1996 has led to considerable changes in the growers' behaviour, which obviously had certain impacts on the labour market dynamics of the sector. For understanding the growers' behavioural pattern, data was collected from select number of small holding farmers—20 each from the three study regions. The selection of the farmers was done giving adequate attention to different size classes of farmers, within the small holding sector. The 360 tappers interviewed in the study are found engaged in a total of 595 plots. As most of the growers are found having single plots, the sample of 60 growers represents around 10 per cent of the total number of growers.

An important characteristic of the growers in the study regions is the predominance of part time farming. More than three-fourth of the growers have additional sources of income other than the cultivation of rubber. These mostly include the earnings from other occupations in which the growers or their family members are engaged. Notwithstanding this, majority of them (about 90 per cent) reported that they have been largely depending on rubber farming as a major source of family income. The unanticipated dip in the market prices and its continuance for a considerably long period has reported to have affected their livelihoods to a greater extent. A setback in the rubber prices means a set back to the general economy of the study regions, whereby the reduction in rubber prices drastically affects not only the income of small growers, but also has multiplier effects on the rural economy. The effect is felt in almost all commercial/trade/business concerns, such as provision stores, cloth merchants, hotel industry, taxi/jeep owners, automobile agencies and service stations, construction industry and so on. All these have generally led to a sluggishness of activities in the local economies during the time of survey. The direct and immediate brunt was, however, borne by two categories, i.e, the growers and tappers in small holding sector. While it is attempted in Chapter 7, to capture the detailed responses of the tappers in terms of livelihood mechanisms and diversification strategies, the present appendix note focuses on the responses of the growers to the price collapse.

Most of the small growers reported that they have drastically reduced the extra-wage monetary support, which had been provided to the tappers prior to the crisis period. For instance, till 1996, more than two-third of the farmers, had given some consumption loans, ranging between Rs. 1000—Rs. 5000, during the rainy season. In some of the study regions, this system had also been assumed the name of 'rainy season advance'. At the time of survey, this system has been on the decline. Only 14 out of the 60 respondents informed that they had given some advance to the tappers during off-season. Similarly, most of the growers reported that they have drastically reduced the level of extra-wage, monetary help given to the tappers during times of contingencies such as disease, marriage, death/birth and educational requirement of children. A few growers also reported that they had stopped the system of providing advance payments against wages, and got into a consensus with the tappers that the wages would be settled at the time of sale of the produce.

Another major change in the farmers' behaviour, in times of crisis, was a massive reduction in the expenditure on crop protection and land development. In several cases, the growers reported that the sudden fall in family income has forced them to reduce the outlay on weeding, manuring and spraying chemicals (e.g. copper oxychloride) and on other plant protection activities. Land development activities (such as bunding, fencing etc.) are also reported to have ceased or minimised by majority of the growers. The postponement of rain-guarding or panel protection is also reported widely as a measure to control the expenditure. These responses are due to the fact that the additional increase in the yield due to these measures in the short run is found to be lower than the expenditure required for continuing these activities. Most of them, though are fully aware of the long-run costs and losses due to inadequate plant protection activities, have no other way than focusing on cost-minimisation efforts. Along side with the dip in rubber prices, it was widely reported that the prices of inputs (both those required for regular tapping—such as acid; and those required for rain-guarding and plant protection) have shot up considerably. In this context, most of the farmers have resorted to either reducing the intensity of tapping or postponement of farm improvement activities.

The cost of labour is the most prominent component of total cost of cultivation. In the absence of a possibility of cutting down the wages considerably, some of the farmers are found tackling the labour cost in an indirect way. This is mainly through extending the interval of tapping and expanding the span of tapping rest. Some of the farmers (8 out of the 60 interviewed) shifted from D/2 pattern to D/3 pattern, which allowed them to reduce the labour cost to some extent. In some cases, the farmers also reported expanding the period of tapping rest by 2-3 weeks mainly to reduce labour use.

The possibility of wage increase in the sector is completely ruled out by most of the growers, until there is a visible revival in the market price of natural rubber. They are found strongly believing that the tappers would not be demanding for wage hikes, as they themselves are aware of the intensity of the crisis. Further, it is also pointed out that the fact that reasonable level of wages were paid to tappers during the period of prosperity, would deter the tappers from raising unrealistic demands for wage rise. This argument has been further supported by the fact that tappers had been continuing in the work without much resistance, despite the non-revision of wages for the past few years.

Many a growers are also found apprehensive about continuing with the crop. Few of them have already contemplated or shifted towards slaughter tapping in their farms, as they do not have any hopes of a revival in product prices in the near future. In two of the plots, slaughter tapping is going on, while few other growers have already decided to switch over to slaughter tapping, from the next season onwards. Some of the respondents are planning to shift over to other crops such as plantain, pineapple, cocoa, vanilla, nutmeg, coconut and betelvine. Though rubber does not allow much scope for intercropping or mixed cropping, as a shock absorbing arrangement, few growers in the locality reported to have planted intercrops such as betelvine, pepper and pineapple in their immature rubber holdings. The logic followed in these cases is to get rid of rubber and continue with the other crop, after observing the market trends for few more months.

In about a dozen cases (one-fifth of the total), the farmers reported that they have reached into 'consensus' with the workers that they would not be paying the full payment due to them, while settling the annual accounts, as their financial position is not that favourable to clear all the dues. It is widely reported that in most of the cases, the workers are found obliging to these pleas rather than resisting it or approaching the trade unions or intermediaries for negotiations. Some of the farmers explained that the growers in these regions are paying lesser amounts of compensation, than earlier, at the time of felling the trees after slaughter tapping. This has been mostly done on the basis of one-to-one agreements between the grower and the tapper.

The worst affected among the growers are those engaged in farming in tiny holdings, and those who depend mostly on income from rubber as the prime source of household survival. This category of growers is found engaged in distress selling of produce and other ways of short-run stabilisation of family income. Selling of improperly dried sheets (without investing time and resources on smoking or drying) at lower prices, and pouring latex directly to collection centres were found as the two prominent ways of distress selling. In 3 cases the growers reported selling improperly dried sheets to the traders, while in 2 other cases the latex has been directly sold. It is pointed out by the growers that they had been doing these in order to avoid investing on the highly risky product and to stabilize the income from the crop, at least for a short-run.

In one of the cases, the grower is found retaining the flow of income at an earlier level, by shifting to slaughter tapping, in a plot where the trees are only 12 years old. In this particular case, the farmer is found desperately retaining the income flow from the plot, which was mainly utilised for his son's education in a professional college. In three cases, the farmers are also found reached into sharecropping arrangements with the tappers, where the total income from the crop is shared between the two on a 50 : 50 basis. The farmers who are engaged in these arrangements opined that the major advantage of this is that they need not bother about arranging wages for the tappers, which itself has become a difficult task during the crisis period.

On the whole, it could be seen that though the growers are the immediate losers due to the price crisis, the burden has been, in many a case, shifted to the tappers without much time lag. The impact of farmers' responses on the workers ranged from the reduction in real wages to long run loss in employment and income.

NOTES

1. A detailed write-up on the crisis and related developments in the rubber sector is provided in Appendix 7.1.
2. In the case of natural rubber, the recession in Indian economy has resulted in lower domestic consumption in recent years. Allowing import of natural rubber, especially at lower import duty at the time when the domestic production is in surplus, slash down the price of Indian rubber drastically.
3. For a detailed discussion on the farmers' responses to the rubber crisis and its labour implications see Appendix 7.2.
4. There is a noticeable decline in the acceptability of the job among youngsters and the existing tappers, which are quite contrary to the situation, prevailed about a decade ago.

8

Summary of Findings and Conclusion

A broader conceptualisation, based on the existing macro level data and literature, suggests that the rural labour market in Kerala is unique *vis-à-vis* the rest of India, in terms of several features such as high degree of unionisation among workers; existence of higher wages, with extreme downward rigidity; higher reservation price of labour; general aversion among job seekers towards agricultural work, with a strong preference for service sector employment; and highly impersonal and institutionalised employer—employee relations. However, of late, there has been an increasing recognition that the universal application of these macro features to all segments of the rural sector may be misleading. Accordingly, it is often argued that the conceptualisation of rural labour markets based on a generic framework, fails to fully explain the dynamics of rural labour market. In this background, the present micro empirical study explores the labour issue and relations in the small holding sector of natural rubber plantations in Kerala.

Summary of Findings

Over the past few decades, the natural rubber cultivation in Kerala has undergone a visible structural transformation, through which the small holding sector has emerged as the prominent segment. A major upshot of this organisational transformation is the emergence and growth of part-time farming, with considerable dependence on hired labour. These paid rubber tappers constituted the major set of respondents for the present study.

The sex-wise segregation of the tappers reveals strikingly skewed distribution of workforce, with considerably lower participation of women, in all study areas. A probing into the poor participation of women in the occupation points to the invisibility of women in tapping. The male tappers are often supported by female members and even children of the family in collecting the latex and coagula, transportation of latex and preparation of rubber sheets. Thus, though the work is carried out collectively, the contributions of women and children remain invisible, as they are neither recognised nor remunerated as assistants.

An interesting revelation of the study is the widespread acceptance of tapping among various social groups, cutting across caste boundaries. People from the socially backward castes are found opting tapping, as it helps to come out of the grips of caste hierarchy. The caste free identity of the occupation is also found attracting people from upper castes. This needs to be seen in a broader context of the widely documented aversion of Keralites to accept 'blue collar' jobs. The general acceptance of the occupation cutting across the caste hierarchies indicates that the shying away of Kerala labour from farm operations is determined by the social status attached to the job within the caste hierarchy.

Tapping is found to be a highly skilled occupation, where the workers require skill and experience to enter the labour market. Normally, tapping skill is acquired through apprenticeship or *via* practicing the operation on other trees with similar bark-width. As improper tapping implies crop loss and permanent damage to the trees, employers are careful in selecting adequately skilled tappers. All these imply entry barriers and higher age of entry into the occupation.

An implication of the structural change in rubber cultivation is the declining employment prospects of the sector, which is determined by the pattern of tapping and the level of tapping task. The lower quantum of tapping task in small holdings makes it impossible for the tapper to ensure a reasonable level of employment from a single holder. Irrespective of the study regions, the average tapping task was found too low to employ a tapper throughout the year. To address this situation, the tappers were found attaching themselves with more than one grower. This 'multiple grower dependency' was visible with some degree of inter-area variations, in all the study regions. This phenomenon of multiple employer status, *prima facie* could be viewed as a situation of enhanced vulnerability and footloose nature of the workforce.

The quantum of employment is inadequate even when the worker relies on multiple growers. Majority of the tappers (77 per cent) are faced with the problem of inadequate tapping task, given the prominence of D/2 pattern of tapping. Of the 595 plots, 72 per cent of tappers were found working with D/2 system, which is followed D/1 pattern (25 per cent). Only 43.6 per cent of respondents are found getting more than 6 month's employment from tapping. The average employment varied drastically across regions within a range of 153-208 days; and with an overall average of 182 days.

Wage payment system in small holdings is based on piece rates, with 95.56 per cent of the respondents employed with piece rate wage contracts. In all the study regions, wage rates were reportedly lower and were found stagnating for the past 5-6 years. Average wage rate was found to be Ps. 27 for all regions together. The stagnation in wages is mainly linked to the crisis in the domestic natural rubber market, consequent to its integration with world natural price movements since the mid 1990s. An examination of the correlation between tapping task and piece rate wages show significant and negative relationships which points towards a situation where tappers are given higher wages to compensate for the lower tapping task and *vice versa.* This broadly reflects the labour retaining mechanisms adopted by small growers to counter skilled labour shortages. The overall situation of low level daily wage earnings from piece rate tapping is quite contrary to the macro scenario of the state which is otherwise known for prevalence of higher wages across most of the rural occupations. The stagnation in wages in tapping, assumes added significance, in the context of rising wages in alternative rural occupations and the cost of living of the workers.

The reduced average annual earnings, during a period of crisis in rubber markets, is found deterring the entry of younger generation into the occupation, thereby leading to some tightness in the labour market. Though the shortage is still in its nascent stage and to some extent could be attributed to the imperfect information and lack of coordination in rural areas, it is likely to become more acute, in view of the reduced preference of younger generation towards tapping on account of prevailing lower and stagnant wages.

Quite contrary to the existing notions of labour market in rural areas the small holding natural rubber farming exhibits marked differences in the labour tying arrangements and labour market characteristics, as opposed to the general agricultural scenario of the state and even to that of the estate sector of rubber plantation. The core parameters of labour contracts in the small holdings such as tenure, wages, extra-wage and non-pecuniary benefits, terms of work, compensation provisions and so on also vary drastically *vis-à-vis* those in the estate sector or rural/agricultural sector as a whole. As against the commonly accepted tendency of increasingly formal, impersonal and often-institutionalised employer-employee interactions in Kerala, with the massive erosion of the patron-client relations, the rubber holdings are mostly characterised with informal and personalised labour contracts.

In all the study regions, contractual arrangements were found informal and unwritten, which is based on a mutual consensus arrived at orally between the growers and tappers. The commencement or renewal of informal work contracts are normally done at the time of commencement of the tapping season, subsequent to the monsoon months or the period of tapping rest, when both the parties clarifies their stands regarding the details of various contractual parameters, such as processes involved in tapping, system of wage payments, rate of wages, bonus, other extra wage benefits, working hours and so on.

A considerable proportion of the respondents (65.7 per cent) reported that they are engaged in annual contracts where the contractual commitment is for a particular tapping season, while the rest have reported working with long-term or permanent contracts. A detailed probing into the nature of permanent contracts, however, revealed that they are no way different from the annual contracts. The perception of 'permanent' status is more or less based on the notion of the workers rather than the legitimacy or social validity of the term. Thus, essentially, all the tappers are found engaged in annual contracts, which are for a particular tapping season. As the renewal of the contract is implicit and are understood both by the growers and the tappers, this act of treating permanent contracts as annual and the tappers as 'temporarily permanent' could be mainly to insulate growers from the risk of long-term commitments and some other adverse implications. The findings indicate the prevalence of long-term contractual associations, though there is a visible resistance by growers in recognising and legalising these arrangements as 'permanent'.

An important feature of the prevailing contractual arrangements in the rubber holdings of Kerala is the interlocking of the tappers and growers through a unique scheme of wage payment, which often assumes the nature of a voluntary system of indebtedness. In all the study regions, the majority of the tappers were found receiving wages in terms of weekly advances, where the norms for fixing the sum include the quantum of work (tapping task); levels of skill and experience of the tapper; years of service with particular grower; and the 'overall reputation' of the tapper in the locality. The settling of these advance amounts is normally done once in a year and the arrears are carried over to the next years' account. This practice of taking advances and carrying forward the arrears to subsequent years was found assuming the form of a voluntary system of indebtedness or bondage.

Interlinked transactions through provision of extra contractual support were found as an effective mode to forge long-term relationship between tappers and growers. The payment of extra wage benefits such as festival advance, bonuses and other sorts of advances are not formally included in the work contract, though these extra wage benefits are provided differently across regions and as per the individual understanding between tappers and growers. Provision of credit was reportedly stronger in all the study regions, prior to the period of rubber crisis. The system of interest free consumption loans and off-season advances with long repayment period were the accepted modes of credit provision. With the crisis in the rubber sector, the extent of such credit availability is highlighted to have declined, though the system is still prevalent.

The unique labour relations and processes in small holding rubber sector suggest that the contractual arrangements in the sector could be understood as a typical agency problem, which is determined by the non-observability of tapper's work effort, inability to decompose the exact contribution of tappers to output and the issue of non-enforceability of contractual terms. As tapping is a regular process, which is carried out throughout the year with a brief period of tapping interval there is an issue of non-observability of tapper's work effort. Diseconomies of small-scale farming make it impossible to introduce paid supervisors, as in the case of estate sector. The growers are also not in a position to decompose or delineate the exact contribution of tappers, as the yield is based on several other exogenous factors such as moisture content in the atmosphere, age of the trees, climatic conditions and so on. Thus, the grower cannot exactly attribute a production loss to the tappers laziness or bad work. All these issues cumulatively lead to the problem of non-enforceability of contractual terms. The strong preference for entertaining long-term contract could be seen as an act to counter the issues arising out of non-observability and non-enforceability in rubber tapping.

The growers who find it difficult to monitor the tappers at work throughout the season are keen to maintain close personal relations with the latter. This is akin to the situation in small scale industries, where due to scale-diseconomies the entrepreneurs often establish personalized relationships with their employees rather than investing resources on stringent monitoring and supervision. The strong preference for devising extra contractual acts of mutual support could be viewed as a mode of personalising labour relations so as to check any kind of shirking and moral hazards. The existence of various forms of extra contractual supports could be seen as strategies for creating personal or moral ties, which ensures desirable levels of work-effort and cover the moral hazard problems. The small rubber holdings further exemplify an agency problem due to 'adverse selection', especially where the principal is not familiar with the characteristics (e.g. ability) of the agent. The growers are found keen in finding out solutions for this issue, as the farm profits, both short run and long run, are closely linked to the quality of work and quantum of work effort provided by the tappers. Since there is heterogeneity of labour, the growers preferentially engage workers whom they know to be better workers. The system of advance payments help the small growers to tie the labour for a fairly long time, and this is more often resorted to address the problems such as adverse selection, where the growers are facing with a relative shortage for tappers (due to unavailability of adequate number of skilled and experienced hands), even when there exists an excess supply of workers in terms of numbers.

Personal ties nurtured through extra wage supports and restricted mobility resulting from the peculiar nature of skill involved in tapping are found delimiting the bargaining capacity of the tappers to bid for wage rise or to resist the withdrawal of support systems. Though the degree of extra wage support and other incentive structures are reported to have reduced considerably during the period of rubber market depression, the tappers find it difficult to negotiate for higher wages or break the contract mainly due to the moral binding arising out of long term personal relations and the perception that wages would increase at any time, if there is any revival in the market price of rubber. The phenomenon of complete absence of resistance towards non-revision of wages for almost 6 years, despite the increases cost of living and relative wages of alternative rural occupations is quite distinct from the overall labour scenario of the state.

The near absence of trade union activities among the tappers could be attributed to the informal and personal ties existing in the sector, which do not leave much space for institutionalised labour relations. Contrary to the overall characteristic of the rural sector and the general agricultural sector, organisational initiatives among the tappers were found at an alarmingly low level. The role of trade unions was found confined to negotiations regarding compensation at times of retrenchment or felling of trees. The rubber tappers in the small and tiny holding sector are also found deprived of the protective provisions of the Plantation Labour Act, 1951, as well as subject to massive exclusion from the benefits from the Rubber Board due to their 'permanently temporary' status.

In the context of declining real wages and reduced employment days, tappers are found coping through the adoption of various adjustment mechanisms, either at the individual level or at the household level. Conscious reductions in the consumption expenditure of the households or an increased dependence on borrowing (from friends and relatives) are found as the initial responses to the shrinking of real earnings by most of the respondents. However, in the context of the continuance of the crisis, these adjustments are found unsustainable, which prompted many tappers to resort to diversify the income base of the households. Due to the peculiarity of the process and seasonality involved in rubber tapping, tappers are normally engaged in a number of income augmenting activities, both in the off-season and along side regular tapping job. About 60 per cent of the tappers are found engaged in some subsidiary income augmenting activities, which include mostly other agricultural work followed by non-farm engagements (including self-employment) and farm work in own homesteads. General work in the rubber holdings itself is found to be one of the prominent sources of supplementary employment to the tappers. The other major forms of farm sector employment included casual and unskilled works such as land preparation, weeding, manuring and pesticide application.

The engagement in other non-farm employment opportunities points towards several built-in flexibilities attached to these supplementary engagements. All these occupations are more less without any stringent time or with a timing that does not conflict with the time requirement in the rubber holdings. Further, many of these self-employment activities were run with complementary involvement of other family members. Yet another way resorted by tappers to supplement the income is to carry out tapping work alongside with their involvement with the other family members or relatives in the traditional jobs such as blacksmithing, carpentry, mat weaving and so on. Though the prominence of farm work in own land was found comparatively lower in all the regions, these activities are found acting as shock absorber in many cases.

The other members of tapper households are also found supplementing the diversification process either by intensifying their involvement in existing engagements or taking up new income generating activities. An important way of augmenting household income is through provision of support to tappers at workplace. Of the various sources of income diversification activities of family member, off-farm work constituted for the largest share, followed by non-farm work and own farm work.

Conclusion and Policy Implications

It is explicit from the findings of the study that the underlying features of labour relations in small holding rubber plantations is quite different from the macro characteristics of the rural labour market of the state. This in turn suggests that there is a need for rethinking generalisations and revisiting some of the stylised facts underlying rural labour dynamics in the state, in the light of sector specific micro level investigations.

Declining employment opportunities for women in agriculture as a whole with the transformations in the crop pattern has been one of the central issues in the development debate of the state. The fact that women's contribution is significant, though invisible, even in a male dominated occupation such as tapping highlights the need for further probing into and mapping of women's unaccounted contribution in the changed economic milieu. This also suggests towards the gaps in the concepts and methodology engaged in capturing women's contribution in economic activity.

Caste free identity of the occupation is yet another aspect which needs to be dissected in the conceptualisation of rural labour dynamics of the state. Tapping like any other agricultural operations is manually demanding and comes well within the 'blue collar farm based jobs'. The acceptability of the occupation irrespective of caste and communal identities suggest that the shying away of Kerala labour from farm operations is determined by the social status attached to the job within the caste hierarchy. Thus it could be argued that, it is the caste identity that determines the entry of job seekers into occupations than the blue-collar status. These points to the strong prominence of caste-based segmentation and rigidities in the rural labour market, despite a long history of radical social and political movements. This also highlights the need for formulating policies that address the mismatches in the labour market in terms of introduction of new occupations and processes that could overcome the caste based hierarchical social ordering.

The existence of low wages and absence of wage revisions for a fairly long period contrasts the sector to the macro setting of the rural economy. The very fact that tappers are deprived of adequate earnings from tapping and even skilled and experienced tappers are unable to earn comparable wages *vis-à-vis* their counterparts in general agriculture indicate that some of the specific issues of the sector deviate considerably from the popular perception and conceptualisation of the rural labour market in Kerala.

The other most important aspect is the near absence of trade unions in the wage setting process, which is quite unanticipated in a state like Kerala, which is otherwise known for institutionalised arrangements in labour relations. The docility and submissiveness of tappers, even during a period of reduction in real earnings is quite contrast to the macro situation, where the workers are otherwise known for militancy and detrimental practices. In this context, the study highlights the need for rationalisation of the wage structure in small holdings and also underlines the desirability of devising feasible policy options, to help the small holding tappers during periods of dwindling real earnings.

A major factor that perpetuates the exploitative labour relations in tapping is the absence of any formal mechanism for wage revision and regulations of other terms of work. Developing local level bipartite and tripartite systems that encourage social dialogue and provide well-defined guidelines could help in improving the conditions of tappers. A major role in this regard is vested with the state. Though at a broader level there are some interventions such as the Plantation Labour Act and the Rubber Board initiated social security measures, these measures exclude the lion share of small holding tappers. The definition employed under the Plantation Labour Act excludes all tappers in small holdings from its protective provisions. The certification from growers stipulated by the Rubber Board in accessing welfare measures is found to deny tappers their eligible benefits as growers are reluctant in recognising the permanent status of tappers. The involvement of worker organisations and local governments in certifying the status could be thought of, to improve the efficacy of the existing schemes.

The failure of trade unions in addressing the unique issues of tappers is another deterrent that weakens the status of tappers. This in turn warrants the need for evolving innovative policies and strategies by trade unions to bring tappers under the umbrella of organised movements. Trade unions and labour-cooperatives could also play central roles in devising measures to overcome the personal bondages arising out of credit linkages, as this would enhance the bargaining strength of tappers to a considerable extent. While doing so, the lessons from existing welfare funds and worker cooperatives in the state could be drawn upon extensively. Yet another important aspect, which requires immediate policy intervention, is the promotion of formal skill development and upgradation and its certification. Recognised skill endowments would empower the workers in effectively bargaining for higher wages and better work conditions.

Further to the above specific interventions, state could play a central role in controlling the price fluctuations the brunt of which is borne by tappers, as in the case of any other export oriented production. Setting floor prices, and intervening in the market by procuring surplus stocks are some of the means that could help controlling the fluctuations in product prices and thus counter possible declines in real earnings. Further, designing of effective welfare measures and amending the Plantation Labour Act to suit the changed circumstances are warranted. Given the definite seasonality and fluctuating employment prospects of rural workers, which is a characteristic feature in all agricultural operations, assuring few days employment through interventions such as rural employment programmes could also be effective in stabilising rural incomes. Such programmes, apart from guaranteeing employment could also raise the reservation price of workers, thereby increasing their bargaining strength. Yet another aspect that warrants immediate attention is the status of data sources on the sector, which is at present poor and extremely scanty. Agencies such as Rubber Board could play a crucial role in this regard. Statistical information on vital aspects such as number of workers, profile of workers, systems of wages and bonus and so on could help a long way in effective policy formulation and welfare intervention.

ANNEXURE-I

Questionnaire I : Tappers

DYNAMICS OF RURAL LABOUR IN KERALA:
A Case Study of Rubber Tappers in Small Holdings

Identification Data

Serial No.
Place of Survey:
Date and Time:

I. Personal Information :

1. Name and Address of the Respondent:

2. Age (in completed years):

3. Sex: Male-1; Female-2

4. Religion: Hindu-1; Christian-2; Muslim-3; Others-4 (Specify)

5. Caste: Upper-1; OBC-2; SC/ST-3; Specify.

6. Marital Status: Single-1; Married-2; Divorced-3; Separated-4

7. Educational Background:
   No formal schooling-1; Primary incomplete-2;
   Primary complete-3; Secondary incomplete-4;

Secondary complete-5; Pre University complete-6; Graduate-7; Post Graduate-8; Others-9 (Specify)

8. Occupational Details:

*Occupational Status**	*Approximate Annual Days of Employment*
Main Occupation ( ) Subsidiary I ( ) Subsidiary II ( )	

* *Occupational Category:* Rubber Tapper-1; Other Agricultural labour-2; Cultivator 3; Self Employed (other than cultivation) 4; Non-farm wage earner-5; Others (specify)-6

9. Family Particulars (including respondent):

Sl. No.	*Relationship to the head*	*Age*	*Sex*	**Educational Status*	***Main Occupation*	*Subsidiary Occupation*

* *Educational Status*: No formal schooling-1; Primary incomplete-2; Primary complete-3; Secondary incomplete-4 ; Secondary complete-5; Pre University complete-6 ; Graduate-7 ; Post Graduate-8, Others (specify)-9

** *Occupational Category:* Rubber Tapper-1; Other Agricultural Labour-2; Cultivator-3; Self Employed (other than cultivation)-4; Non farm wage earner-5; Salaried Work-6; Student-7; Unemployed-8, Others (specify)-9.

10. Occupation of father?
11. Occupation of mother?

12. If your parents were not rubber tappers, why did you decide to move out of your parent's occupation? Explain :

13. Do you own house? Yes-1; No-2

14. Do you or your family members own land? Yes-1; No-2

15. If Yes,
    (a) Size (in Acres):   (b) Cultivated Area:
    (c) Fallow Area: (d) Crops Grown:

16. Do you have rubber trees in your holdings?
    Yes-1;   No-2

17. If Yes,
    (a) No. of trees   (b) Age of trees
    (c) Tapping Arrangement

II. Employment Particulars

18. Status of Employment: Full time-1; Part time-2

19. If part time, what is your main occupation or engagement?

20. Details of Employment Across Plots:

Plot No.	Area		The processes carried out*	Quantum of Work		Schedule of Work in the plot	Type of Tapping (D/1, D/2, D/3, Slaughter)	No. of workers (including you) in the plot	Average annual days of employment	Service Experience in the plot(in months)	Type of Contract**
	In Acre	No. of Trees		Hrs	No. of Trees						

* The processes carried out: Tapping-1; Tapping and Collection of Latex-2; Tapping, Latex Collection and Preparation of Sheets-3; Tapping, Latex Collection, Sheet Preparation and Sale of Sheets-4

** Type of Contract: Permanent-1; Temporary-2.

21. Why did you decide to work as a rubber tapper?
    (i) Flexibility of Working Hours
    (ii) Part-time Engagement
    (iii) Attractive Wages
    (iv) Higher Social Status
    (v) Other (Specify)
22. Who helped you to get the job?
    (i) Friends/Village Member
    (ii) Relatives
    (iii) Labour Contractor
    (iv) Others (specify)
23. Approximate number of days of tapping during the last 1 month:

24. Do you find any seasonality in employment? Explain:

25. Specify the Peak and Lean Seasons of Employment:
    (i) Peak Period:
    (ii) Lean Period:

26. If your work is seasonal what is your off-season occupation?

27. Approximate number of days of employment (both tapping and other work) during the last one year:

28. Average hours of work per day, in rubber tapping and related operations:

29. Do you get any off-season allowance from your employer? If yes, give details:

30. How did you acquire the skill of tapping?
    (i) Learning by doing; (ii) Formal Training;
    (iii) Informal Internship

31. If formally trained, explain the following:
    (i) Organisation from which training is obtained:

(ii) Duration of training:
(iii) The processes in which training was imparted:

32. How long did you take for acquiring skill?
In terms of months:
In terms of number of trees tapped:

33. What are the processes in which you were involved, at the time of entry into the job?

34. Do you think that you have acquired certain skills from the present job?

35. Do you consider this skill as an asset? (or as a restriction to your switching over to another job?)

36. Do you own your work implements?

37. If Yes, What are the work implements you possess?

38. What are the work implements you do not possess?

III. Wages, Bonus and other Benefits

39. What is the system of wage payment?
(i) Piece Rate; (ii) Time Rate; (iii) Product Share

40. If piece rate, how much wages do you receive:
(i) Per tree:
(ii) Per sheet:

41. If product share, what is the existing ratio?

42. Total Earnings received from rubber during:
(i) Last month:
(ii) Normal months:
(iii) Peak months:

43. Frequency of payment of wages
(i) Daily:

(ii) Weekly
(iii) Monthly

44. If time rate, average wage:
    Hourly:
    Daily:
    Weekly:
    Monthly:
45. Explain the process and mechanisms of wage fixation and revision?
46. Rank the following factors according to their importance in wage revision:
    - Trade unions
    - Product prices
    - Nature of work
    - Cost of living
    - Productivity
    - Work Intensity
    - Relative Wages
47. Do you think that wages of rubber tappers are really linked to product price?
48. Is there any difference in wages in terms of years of service, experience or degree of skill in the work? If Yes, Explain.
49. Do you think you get reasonable wages? Justify your answer.
50. State the year of last 3 wage revisions:

Time	*Wages Per Tree*	*Proportion of* Sheets	*Time Rate*	*How did you get the wage revision**
Currently				
Previous revision (......................)				
Revision before that (......................)				

* Mechanism of Wage Revision: (i) Organised Collective Bargaining; (ii) Tacit Collective Bargaining; (iii) Due to Statutory Provisions and Government Intervention.

51. Is there any gender-wise difference in wages? If Yes, Explain:

52. Are you entitled to bonus? (i) Yes; (ii) No

53. If yes, give details
    Timing:
    Amount:
    Calculation norms:
54. What is the mechanism of bonus revision?

55. Do Trade Unions have a role in bonus fixation and revision? Explain;

56. What are the other entitlements over and above wages and bonus?
    - Pension: Yes /No—Details
    - Maternity Benefits: Yes/No—Details
    - Medical Allowance: Yes/No—Details
    - Educational Allowance: Yes/No—Details
    - Other Benefits (Specify):—Details
57. Are you entitled to leaves? If Yes, give details:
    No. of leaves permitted with wages:
    No. of leaves permitted without wages:
58. Approximate number of leaves availed by you during the previous year?

59. Do you receive any compensatory allowance during off-season? If yes, give details.

60. In case of retrenchment or slaughter tapping what is the legitimate/conventional compensation available?

61. What are the norms in calculating the compensation?

IV. Legal Protection and Welfare Schemes

62. Do you know about the minimum wages for rubber tappers? (i) Yes; (ii) No

63. If Yes, explain your understanding:

64. Are you aware of the legal protections of Plantation Labour Act, 1951?

65. If yes, do you receive any benefits of PLA? Explain.

66. Are you a beneficiary of the labour welfare schemes of Rubber Board? (i) Yes; (ii) No

67. If yes, explain the benefits

68. Which are the other agencies that provide specific welfare schemes or programmes for rubber tappers? What are their various schemes?

69. Rank the following agencies/organisations according to your utility:
    - Central Government
    - State Government
    - Rubber Board
    - Trade Unions
    - NGOs (give examples)
    - Voluntary Organisations (specify)
70. Do you think that the rubber tappers are legally and socially protected because of the legal provisions and welfare schemes of the above-mentioned agencies?

71. Do you think that the legal protection to the workers is adequate? (i) Yes; (ii) No

72. If Yes/No, Justify your answer.

73. What are the policy prescriptions that you can suggest to improve the welfare situation?

V. Labour Tying Arrangements and Contracting Practices

[*Note*: In case of multiple plots all informations need to be collected separately for each plot]

74. Nature of Contract:
(i) Permanent; (ii) Annual/Seasonal

75. How long have you been employed with the present employer?

76. How did you get into the contract?
(i) Through agent; (ii) Through relatives; (iii) Directly; (iv) Through another worker;
(v) Through Trade Union; (vi) Others (specify)

77. If your engagement is through any of the above-mentioned intermediaries, what are the conditions for getting the job (e.g., union membership, payment of premium etc.)

78. Are you tied to any employer? If so, details of period, payment terms, reasons, its implications etc.

79. Are you free to work with any other employer? If not, why?

80. Does your contract imply engagement of your family member, as a condition (in tapping or in any other type of labour for the employer). If yes, give details:

81. Give details of unpaid work(s), if any, (performed by you or your family member) for the employer.

82. Give details of extra contractual helps from the employer:
(i) Consumption Loans·
(ii) Contingency loans and grants (e.g. Marriage, Child birth, Disease etc.)
(iii) Food; (iv) Dress;

(v) Recommendation (e. g. Admission of Children in College, in getting services of Doctor etc.) (vi) Other (Specify)

83. Are you emotionally attached to your employer? If Yes, Why?
84. Do you agree that work relations are becoming increasingly impersonal, compared to your elders' generation?

85. Did you ever have any conflict with your employer? If yes, give details.

86. Have you ever proposed wage revision? If yes what was the response? If No, the reason for not proposing wage revision?

87. Are you in debt now? (i) Yes; (ii) No

88. If yes, give details:
    (i) Amount:
    (ii) From whom the loan is obtained:
    (iii) Reason for Indebtedness:

89. If there is any loan from the employer, do you think that it acts as a bondage in employment ? Give details.

VI. Trade Union/Organisational Aspects

90. Are you a member of a Trade Union? If Yes, Which union? Specify if the union is affiliated to any of the political parties.
91. History of Union Activities

Name of the Trade Union	Positions held, if any	Period	If left, reason for leaving

92. Briefly state your role in trade union related activities.

93. Have you attended any study/labour camps? If yes, state the details (organiser, period, purpose and comments on effectiveness).

94. Have you participated in any strike or worker protest? If yes, state reason, duration of strike, the outcome etc.

95. What is your opinion about the efficacy of trade union movement in your region in protecting rubber tappers' interests? Explain your answer.

96. Details of the trade unions for tappers in your locality (including your union) in the order of prominence

Name of Trade Union	Approximate Y ear of Starting in the locality	Approximate Strength	Approximate % share in unionized workers	Major Achievements

97. Briefly explain your Knowledge about evolution of Trade Unionism in your occupation in the area. Also state problems encountered in unionism with illustrative cases, if any?

98. Role of Trade Unions in fixing the Wages?
    (i) Passive; (ii) Active; (iii) Active in Crucial revisions
99. Explain and elaborate the above answer:

100. Who heads your union?
    (i) In the locality: (i) Political Leader; (ii) Worker
    (ii) In the State Level: (i) Political Leader; (ii) Worker
101. Explain the Major Merits and Demerits of your trade union.
    (i) Merits:

    (ii) Demerits:

102. Are you active in politics: (i) Yes; (ii) No

103. If yes, give details:

VII. Migration and Work History Profile

104. Place of birth:

105. Do you work in the locality around your permanent residence ? If No, give details:
    (i) Distance from permanent residence;
    (ii) Reasons for coming here;

106. When did you first leave your permanent place of residence in search of job?
    Month: Year:

107. When was your first entry to wage work and what was your first occupation?
    Year:
    Occupation:

108. Causes of Entry into labour market for the first time?
    (i) Indebtedness
    (ii) Need for supplementing the family income
    (iii) Increased family obligations
    (iv) Landlessness
    (v) Lack of Property
    (vi) School drop out

109. How long have you been into tapping?

110. Previous employment details:

Occupation	*Job Category	Nature of job	Year of Working	Experience (in months)	Skills required	Average Working hrs	Wage rate (8 hrs)	**Reason for leaving the job
Previous I								
Previous II								
Previous III								

* *Job Category:* (i) Rubber Tapper /Plantation labour; (ii) Other Agricultural labour; (iii) Self Employed other than agriculture; (iv) Non farm wage earner; (v) Salaried Job; (vi) Student; (vii) Inactive; (viii) Unemployed, (ix) Others (specify).

** *The Reason for leaving the previous job:* (i) Unemployed and Searching employment; (ii) Better earnings; (iii) Better work conditions; (iv) Accompany family; (v) Retrenched from previous job; (vi) Not Applicable; (vii) Others (specify)

VIII: Perception on the Changing Rubber Scenario

111. Do you think that the rubber holdings are going through a crisis period?
     (i) Yes; (ii) No

     (i) If Yes, Justify:

112. Did you experience any wage cut due to the decline of rubber price in the market?
     (i) Yes; (ii) No
     (i) If yes, Explain:

113. Do you think that the employment and wages in the sector will further decline?
     (i) Yes; (ii) No
114. If yes, what is your future plan?

115. What did the government do to protect the interest of the workers during the crisis?

116. Do you think the government action was adequate? Justify and Explain.

117. What did the trade unions do in this regard?

118. Do you think the trade unions' action was adequate? Justify and Explain.

119. What section is the most affected due to the crisis, in your opinion:
     (i) Large and Medium Growers
     (ii) Petty Holdings
     (iii) Tappers and other workers.
120. What were the responses of growers to the crisis?
121. How do you assess the attitude and responses of the growers? Explain in detail.

122. What is your opinion on the adequacy of social security to workers? Explain.
123. What are your suggestions to improve the scene?

IX: Livelihood Diversification

124. Do you think that the crisis in the rubber economy has affected your income and standard of living? Explain your answer.
125. In the event of reduced income or stagnation of wages how did you stabilize your earnings?
   (i) Increased debt—Give details.
   (ii) Reducing family expenditures in food, clothing, education, etc.—Give details.
   (iii) By increasing the number of trees—Give details.
   (iv) Taking up subsidiary and multiple occupations—Give details.
126. How do your family members support in maintaining the income?
   (i) Help in latex collection and preparation—Give details.
   (ii) Taking up self-employment such as cattle rearing—Give details.
   (iii) Entry of family members into regular employment—Give details.
127. How did the employer help you during the crisis to sustain your standard of living?
128. In the event of continuance of crisis, what are your future strategies for livelihood? Explain.

ANNEXURE-II

Questionnaire II: Growers

DYNAMICS OF RURAL LABOUR IN KERALA
A Case Study of Rubber Tappers in Small Holdings

Identification Data:

Serial No.
Place of Survey:
Date and Time:

I. Personal Identification:

1. Name and Address:
2. Age:
3. Sex:
4. Main Occupation:
5. Subsidiary Occupation:
6. Details of other earning members in the family:
7. Sources of income other than rubber cultivation:
8. Total earnings of other members of the family:

II. Cultivation Particulars:

9. Details of land owned:
   (a) Total Land: (b) Cultivated:
   (c) Non-Cultivated: (d) Crops Cultivated:
10. Details of Rubber Holding (s):
   (a) No. of Trees: (b) Age of Trees:
   (c) Approx. Area:

11. Is Rubber cultivated as a Mixed Crop? (i) Yes (ii) No
    (a) If yes, give details of other crops grown:
    (b) If intercropping is followed, state whether certain operations (such as weeding and pesticide application) are done jointly. If yes, briefly, explain:
12. Calendar of operations during mature period

Operation	*Month(s)*	*Remarks, if any (If there is any change in the calendar recently, please mention along with reason)*
Tapping		
Panel Protection		
Rain guarding		
Weeding—I Round		
Weeding—II Round		
Manuring—I Round		
Manuring—II Round		
Spraying (e.g. Copper Oxychloride)		
Other Plant Protection Activities (specify)		
Others (specify)		
Tapping Rest		

13. Specify your tree equivalent of an acre
    1 Acre = trees
14. How long it will take a rubber tree to provide yield?

15. The type of tapping followed in your holding? D/1, D/2, D/3 slaughter
    (a) Why are you following the particular type of tapping?
        (i) As per instructions of the Rubber Board
        (ii) Convenience of the worker
        (iii) To reduce labour Cost
        (iv) Some other reason (specify)

16. Your Annual Labour Requirement (for 1 Acre=100 cents): For mature phase

Item	*Number of Mandays Required*	*Approximate operation-wise wages paid for unit labour for a day*
Weeding		
Manuring		
Spraying (e.g. Copper Oxychloride)		
Other plant protection activities (specify)		
Tapping and Processing (specify whether D/1, D/2, D/3 Slaughter)		
Rainguarding		
Panel Protection		
Other (specify)		
Total		

17. Your operation-wise Labour Requirement (for one acre): During Immature Period

Item	*Number of mandays required per acre*	
	First Year	*Subsequent year of the Immature Phase*
Clearing		
Terracing and Soil Conservation Activities		
Filling and Planting		
Fixing Shade baskets, Propping and Lime Washing		
Pruning and Branch Induction		
Weeding and Mulching		
Manuring		
Plant Protection		
Cover Crop Establishment and Upkeep		
Drainage and Miscellaneous Work		
Boundary protection, Fencing and Footpath Maintenance		
Security		
Other (specify)		
Total		

18. What is the going wage rate for 'general work' in rubber holdings?

III. Contractual Particulars; Organisational and General Aspects

19. What is the extra wage benefit provided by you to your worker ?

20. How do you ensure that your worker work properly for you ?

21. Do you prefer same workers to continue for several years in your holdings? Justify your answer.

22. Will you give certification to the worker in your holdings? If not, explain why?

23. What are the different ways in which a worker could fool you (e.g. avoid working, damaging the trees, stealing the products, etc.)

24. How do you avoid such actions of the tappers?

25. What is your remark on trade unionism among tappers in region?

26. Have you had any conflict with any of your worker or worker unions in the past? If yes, explain.

27. Do you prefer a migrant labour to local labour or vice versa? Justify your answer?

28. What is your opinion regarding the crisis in rubber sector and the possible remedial measures?

IV. Responses to Crisis

29. Have you dropped or reduced the intensity of any of the operation to minimise the cost of cultivation due to the increased non-profitability of rubber cultivation in recent years? If yes, explain (e.g. Moved from D/1 to D/2 or D/3; Stopped Tapping; Dropped Manuring etc.)

30. Do you think that the crisis in the rubber sector has led to some change in terms of the labour contract?

31. How did you handle issues related to wage revision, extra wage support and bonus during the period of crisis?

32. What is your opinion regarding the wage stagnation and the possibility of its revision in the upward direction?

33. Has the stagnation in wages brought in any decrease in labour supply? Explain?

34. In case of continuance of crisis for some more years what are your strategies in terms of:

(a) Continuing rubber cultivation—
- Investing on plant protection and soil development
- Maintaining the current wage
- Continuing with the extra-wage support
- Type of contract
- Type of tapping

(b) Shifting to other crops,
(c) Selling of land,
(d) Any other strategy? Explain.

Bibliography

Acharya, S. (1989): 'Agricultural Wages in India: A Disaggregated Analysis', *Indian Journal of Agricultural Economics,* Vol. 44, No. 2.

Akerlof, G. (1984): 'Gift Exchange and Efficiency Wage: Four Views,' *American Economic Review,* Vol. 74, No. 2.

Akerlof, G. A. and J. L. Yellen (ed.) (1986): 'Efficiency Wage Models of the Labour Market', Cambridge University Press, Cambridge.

Albin, Alice (1990): 'Manufacturing Sector in Kerala: Comparative Study of its Growth and Structure', *Economic and Political Weekly,* Vol. 25, No. 37.

Arrow, Kenneth J. (1985): 'The Economics of Agency', in Pratt J. and Zeckhauser, R. (ed.), "Principals and Agents: The Structure of Business", Harvard Business School Press, Boston.

Baby, A.A (1996): 'Trends in Agricultural Wages in Kerala, 1960-1990', *Monograph Series,* Centre for Development Studies, Trivandrum.

Baby, A.A (2003): 'The Pattern of Wage Differentials of Rural, Urban Skilled and Unskilled Workers: A Local Level Approach to Study the Wage Bargaining', Mimeo, Kerala Research Programme on Local Level Development, CDS, Trivandrum.

Bardhan, K. (1973): 'Factors Affecting Wage Rates for Agricultural Labour', *Economic and Political Weekly,* Vol. 8, No. 26.

Bardhan, K. (1984): 'Work Patterns and Social Differentiation: Rural Women of West Bengal', in Binswanger and Rosenzweig (ed.), "Contractual Arrangements, Employment, and Wages in Rural Labour Markets in Asia", Yale University Press, New Haven.

Bardhan, K. (1989); 'Poverty, Growth and Rural Labour Markets in India', *Economic and Political Weekly,* Vol. 24, No. 12

Bardhan, P.K. (1977): 'Variations in Forms of Tenancy in a Peasant Economy', *Journal of Development Economics,* Vol. 42.

Bardhan, P.K. (1980): 'Interlocking Factor Markets and Agrarian Development: A Review of Issues', *Oxford Economic Papers,* Vol. 32, No. 1.

Bardhan, P.K. (1983): 'Labour-Tying in a Poor Agrarian Economy: A Theoretical and Empirical Analysis', *Quarterly Journal of Economics,* Vol. 98, No. 3.

Bardhan, P.K. (1994): 'Land, Labour and Rural Poverty: Essays in Development Economics', Columbia University Press, New York.

Bardhan, P.K. and Rudra, A. (1981): 'Terms and Conditions of Labour Contracts in Agriculture Results of a Survey in West Bengal', *Oxford Bulletin of Economics and Statistics,* Vol. 43.

Bardhan, P.K. and Srinivasan, T.N. (1971): 'Crop Sharing Tenancy in Agriculture: A Theoretical and Empirical Research', *American Economic Review,* Vol. 61, No. 1.

Bardhan, P.K. (1979): 'Agricultural Development and Land Tenancy in a Peasant Economy: A Theoretical and Empirical Analysis', *American Journal of Agricultural Economics,* Vol. 61, No. 1.

Bardhan, P.K. (1981): 'Terms and Conditions of Labour Contracts in Agriculture: Results of a Survey in West Bengal, 1979', *Oxford Bulletin of Economics and Statistics,* Vol. 43, No. 1.

Becker, G.S. and Srinivasan, T.N. (1985), 'Some Salient Features of Tenancy Contracts, Commodity Prices and Wages: A Comparison of Andhra Pradesh, Bihar, and Punjab.' Mimeo, World Bank, Washington, DC.

Becker, Gary S. (1974): 'A Theory of Social Interactions', *Journal of Political Economy,* Vol. 82, No. 6.

Becker, Gary S. (1976): 'Altruism, Egoism and Genetic Fitness: Economics and Sociology', *Journal of Economic Literature,* Vol. 3, No. 14.

Bell, C. and Srinivasan, T.N. (1989): 'Interlinked Transactions in Rural Markets An Empirical Study of Andhra Pradesh, Bihar and Punjab', *Oxford Bulletin of Economics and Statistics,* Vol. 51, No. l.

Bhalla, S. (1979): 'Real Wages of Agricultural Labourers in Punjab, 1961-77: A Preliminary Analysis', *Economic, and Political Weekly,* Vol. 14, No. 26.

Bhalla, S. (1993): 'The Dynamics of Wage Determination and Employment Generation in Indian Agriculture', *Indian Journal of Agricultural Economics,* Vol. 48, No. 3.

Bharadwaj, Krishna (1987): 'Wages in Classical Economics' in Eatwell, John; Millgate, Murray and Newman, Peter (ed.) "The New Palgrave: A Dictionary of Economics", The MacMillan Press Limited, London.

Bharadwaj, Krishna (1989): 'On the Formation of the Labour Markets in Rural Asia', Centre for Economic Studies and Planning, Jawaharlal Nehru University, New Delhi.

Bhattacharya, Neeladri, (2004): 'Labour Histories: Agrarian Labour and Colonialism', *NLI Research Study Series,* No. 49. V.V. Giri National Labour Institute, NOIDA

Binswanger *et al.,* (1984): 'Common Features and Contrasts in Labour Relations in the Semi-Arid Tropics of India' in Binswanger and Rosenzweig (ed.), "Contractual Arrangements, Employment, and Wages in Rural Labour Markets in Asia", Yale University Press, New Haven.

Binswanger, H. and Rosenzweig, M. (1984): 'Contractual Arrangements, Employment and Wages in Rural Labour Markets in Asia', Yale University Press, New Haven.

Blanchflower *et al.* (1990): 'Insider Power in Wage Determination', *Economica,* Vol. 57, No. 226.

Braverman, A. and Srinivasan, T.N. (1981): 'Credit and Sharecropping in Agrarian Societies', *Journal of Development Economics,* Vol. 9, No. 3.

Breman, J. (1974): 'Patronage and Exploitation: Changing Agrarian Relations in South Gujarat, India', University of California Press, Berkeley.

Breman, J. (1993): 'Beyond Patronage and Exploitation', Oxford University Press, New Delhi.

Brewster, J.M. (1950), 'The Machine Process in Agriculture and Industry', *Journal of Farm Economics*, Vol. 32, No.1.

Burger, K.; Haridasan, V.; Smit, H.P.; Unni, R.G. and Zant, W. (1995): *Indian Rubber Economy: History, Analysis and Policy Perspectives*, Manohar Publishers, New Delhi.

Carney, D. (1998): 'Implementing the Sustainable Rural Livelihoods Approach', in Carney (ed.), *Sustainable Rural Livelihood: What Contribution Can We Make?* Department for International Development, London.

Cheung, Steven N.S. (1969): *The Theory of Share Tenancy*, University of Chicago Press, Chicago.

Datt, G. (1996): *Bargaining Power, Wages and Employment: An Analysis of Agricultural Labour Markets in India*, Sage Publishers, New Delhi.

Davies, S. and Hossain (1997): 'Livelihood Adaptation, Public Action and Civil Society: A Review of Literature', *IDS Working Paper*, No. 57, Institute of Development Studies, Brighton.

Economic and Political Weekly (1997), 'Farm Workers' Agitation: Return to Politics of Confrontation', *Economic and Political Weekly*, Vol. 32, Nos. 33 and 34.

Ellis, Frank (1998): 'Household Strategies and Rural Livelihood Diversification: Survey Article', *Journal of Development Studies*, Vol. 35, No. 1.

Ellis, Frank (2000): *Rural Livelihoods and Diversity in Developing Countries*, Oxford University Press, New York.

Eswaran, M. and Kotwal, A. (1985): 'A Theory of Contractual Structure in Agriculture', *American Economic Review*, Vol. 75, No. 3.

Fine, Ben (1998): *Labour Market Theory: A Constructive Reassessment*, Routledge Publishers, London.

Franke, Richard W. and Chasin, Barbara H. (1997): 'Power to the Malayalee People', *Economic and Political Weekly*, Vol. 32, No. 48.

Franke, Richard W. and Chasin, Barbara H. (2000): 'Is the Kerala Model Sustainable? Lessons from the Past, Prospects for the Future', in Parayil, Govindan (ed.) *Kerala: The Development Experience—Reflections on Sustainability and Replicability*, Zed Books, London and New York.

Franke, Richard W. (1998): 'Kerala: A Valid Alternative to the New World Order', *Bulletin of Concerned Asian Scholars*, Vol. 30, No. 4.

George, K.T. (1999): 'The Natural Rubber Sector: Emerging Issues in the 1990s' in Prakash, B.A. (ed.) *Kerala's Economic Development: Issues and Problems*, Sage Publications, New Delhi.

George, K.K (1998): 'Historical Roots of Kerala Model and its Present Crisis', *Bulletin of Concerned Asian Scholars*, Vol. 30, No. 4.

George, K.K. (1993): 'Limits to Kerala Model of Development: An Analysis of Fiscal Crisis and its Implications', *Monograph Series*, Centre for Development Studies, Trivandrum.

Government of India (1968): *Report of the Rubber Small Holdings Economics Enquiry Committee*, Ministry of Commerce, Rubber Board, Kottayam.

Government of India (2004): *Wage Rates in Rural India, 2002-03*, Ministry of Labour, Labour Bureau, Shimla, Chandigarh.

Government of Kerala (2001): *Labour Policy 2001*, Department of Public Relations, Trivandrum.

Government of Kerala (2002): *Economic Review 2001-2002*, State Planning Board, Trivandrum.

Government of Kerala (2003): *Economic Review 2002-2003*, State Planning Board, Trivandrum.

Halliburton, Murphy (1998): 'Suicide: A Paradox of Development in Kerala'. *Economic and Political Weekly*, Vol. 33, Nos. 36 and 37.

Hansen, B. (1966): 'Marginal Productivity Wage Theory and Subsistence Wage Theory in Egyptian Agriculture', *Journal of Development Studies*, Vol. 2.

Harris, Milton and Raviv, Artur (1978): 'Some Results on Incentive Contracts with Applications to Education and Employment, Health Insurance, and Law Enforcement', *American Economic Review*, Vol. 68, No. 1.

Harris, Milton and Raviv, Artur (1979): 'Optimal Incentive Contracts with Imperfect Information', *Journal of Economic Theory*, Vol. 20, No. 2.

Hayami, Yujiro and Otsuka, Keijiro (1993): *The Economics of Contract Choice: An Agrarian Perspective,* Clarendon Press, Oxford.

Heller, Patrick (1995): 'From Class Struggle to Class Compromise: Redistribution and Growth in a South Indian Case', *Journal of Development Studies,* Vol. 31, No. 5.

Heller, Patrick (1999): *The Labour of Development: Workers in the Transformation of Capitalism in Kerala, India,* Cornell University Press, Ithaca, New York.

Heller, Patrick (2000): 'Social Capital and the Developmental State: Industrial Workers in Kerala', in Parayil, Govindan (ed.) *Kerala: The Development Experience—Reflections on Sustainability and Replicability,* Zed Books, London and New York.

Heller, Patrick. (1996): 'Social Capital as Product of Class Mobilization and State Intervention: Industrial Workers in Kerala, India'. *World Development,* Vol. 24.

Heller, Patrick. (1998): 'Problematising the Kerala Model'. *Bulletin of Concerned Asian Scholars,* Vol. 30, No. 3.

Holmstrom, B.(1979): 'Moral Hazard and Observability', *Bell Journal of Economics,* Vol. 71, No. 2.

Isaac, Thomas T.M and Tharakan, Michael (1986): 'Sree Narayana Movement in Travancore. 1938-1939: A Study of Social Basis and Ideological Reproduction', *Working Paper,* No. 214, Centre for Development Studies, Trivandrum.

Isaac, Thomas T.M and Tharakan, Michael (1995): 'Kerala: Towards a New Agenda' *Economic and Political Weekly,* Vol. 30, Nos. 31 and 32.

Isaac, Thomas T.M (1995): 'Kerala: Towards a New Agenda'. *Economic and Political Weekly,* Vol. 30, Nos. 31 and 32.

Isaac, Thomas T.M; Franke, Richard W. and Raghavan, Pyarelal. (1998): 'Democracy at Work in an Indian Industrial Cooperative: The Story of Kerala Dinesh Beedi', Cornell University Press, Ithaca, N.Y.

Isaac, Thomas T.M. (1982): 'Class Struggle and Structural Changes: Coir Mat and Matting Industry in Kerala: 1950-1980'. *Economic and Political Weekly,* Vol. 17, No. 31.

Isaac, Thomas T.M. (1985), 'From Caste to Class Consciousness: Alleppey Coir Workers during Inter-War Period', *Economic and Political Weekly*, Vol. 20, No. 4.

Jeffrey, Robin (1992): 'Politics, Women and Well-Being, How Kerala Became 'A Model', London: Macmillan.

Jha, Pravin (1997): 'Agricultural Labour in India', Vikas Publishing House Private Limited, New Delhi.

Jose, A.V. (1978): 'Real Wages, Employment, and Income of Agricultural Labourers', *Economic and Political Weekly*, Vol. 13, No. 12.

Kannan, K.P. (1994): 'Levelling Up Or Levelling Down? Labour Institutions and Economic Development in India', *Economic and Political Weekly*, Vol. 29, No. 30.

Kannan, K.P. (1998): 'Political Economy of Labour and Development in Kerala'. *Economic and Political Weekly*, Vol. 33, No. 52.

Kannan, K.P. (2003): 'Social Dialogue in the Informal Sector: The Kerala Experience of Welfare Funds', in Sivananthiran, A. and Retnam, Venkata, C.S. (ed.) "Best Practices in Social Dialogue", ILO and IIRA, New Delhi.

Kikuchi, Masao, and Hayami, Yujiro (1980), 'Technology and Labour Contract: Two Systems of Rice Harvesting in the Philippines', *Journal of Comparative Economics*, Vol. 4, No. 4.

Krishnan T.N (1991): 'Wages, Employment and Output in Interrelated Labour Markets in an Agrarian Economy: A Study of Kerala' *Economic and Political Weekly*, Vol. 26, No. 26.

Kumar, Krishna and Jacob, Jom (2003): 'Rubber Sector in the Liberalised Economy: Developments in the NR Market in Retrospect', *Indian Rubber Journal*, Vol. 72.

Kumar, Suresh (1993): 'Political Evolution in Kerala, Travancore 1859-1938', Phoenix Publishing House, New Delhi.

Kurien, John (2000): 'The Kerala Model: Its Central Tendency and the Outlier', in Parayil, Govindan (ed.) *Kerala: The Development Experience—Reflections on Sustainability and Replicability*, Zed Books, London and New York.

Kurien, P.K. (2001): *"Sub-Marginal Rubber Cultivation: A Study of Livelihood Issues of Beneficiaries of 'Rubber to Poor' Project of Malanad Development Society, Kanjirappally"*, *Discussion Paper*, Kerala Research Programme on Local Level Development, CDS, Trivandrum.

Labour Bureau: *'Rural Labour Enquiry Report'*, Various Issues, Labour Bureau, Shimla, Chandigarh.

Lalithakumari, E. and Jacob, Jom (2000): 'Natural Rubber Industry in India: An Overview', in George, P.J. and Jacob, Kuruvila (ed.), *Natural Rubber: Agro-management and Crop Processing*, Rubber Research Institute of India, Kottayam.

Leibenstein, H. (1957): *Economic Backwardness and Economic Growth*, Wiley, New York.

Leiten, G.K. (2002): 'The Human Development Puzzle in Kerala', *Journal of Contemporary Asia*, Vol. 32, No. 1.

Lekshmi, S. and George, Tharian K. (2003): 'Expansion of Natural Rubber Cultivation in Kerala: An Exploratory Analysis, *Indian Journal of Agricultural Economics*, Vol. 58, No. 2.

Levinthal, Daniel, (1988): 'A Survey of Agency Models of Organisations', *Journal of Economic Behaviour and Organisation*, Vol. 9, No. 2.

Lindbeck, A. and Snower, Dennis J. (1988): *The Insider-outsider Theory of Employment and Unemployment*, MIT Press, Cambridge.

Lindberg, Anna (2001): *Experience and Identity: A Historical Account of Class, Caste and Gender among Cashew Workers of Kerala, 1930-2000*, Lund University, Washington D.C.

Mahesh, R. (2002): 'Labour Mobility in Rural Areas: A Village Level Study', *Discussion Paper*, No. 48, Kerala Research Programme on Local Level Development, CDS, Trivandrum.

Malik, P.L. (2003): *Industrial Law*, Eighteenth Edition, Eastern Book Company, Lucknow.

Mirlees, J.A. (1975): 'A Pure Theory of Underdeveloped Economies' in Reynolds (ed.) *Agriculture in Development Theory*, Yale University Press, New Haven.

Mohapatra, Prabhu P. (1999): 'Situating the Renewal: Reflections on Labour Studies in India', *Working Paper*, No. 2. (Labour History Series), V.V. Giri National Labour Institute, NOIDA.

Nair, M.K.S. (1997): 'Rural Labour Market in Kerala: Small Holder Agriculture and Labour Market Dynamics', *Economic and Political Weekly*, Vol. 32, No. 35.

Nandamohan, V. (1994): 'Recent Trends in the Industrial Growth of Kerala', in Prakash, B.A (ed.), *Kerala's Economy: Performance, Problems, Prospects*, Sage, New Delhi.

Narayana. D. and Nair, K.N. (1989): 'Heterogeneity, Mobility and Dynamics of Contractual Arrangements in the Agricultural Labour Market in an Irrigated District', *Working Paper*, No. 230, Centre for Development Studies, Trivandrum.

National Sample Survey Organisation (2001): 'Employment and Unemployment Situation in India, 1999-2000', NSS Fifty-fifth Round (July 1999-June 2000), *NSS Report No 458*, NSSO, New Delhi.

Neetha N. (2003): *Institutional Choice in Irrigation: A Case Study of Distribution in a Command Area in Kerala*, Ph.D. Thesis, Jawaharlal Nehru University, New Delhi and Centre for Development Studies, Thiruvananthapuram.

Newberry, David M.G. and Stiglitz, Joseph E. (1979): 'Sharecropping, Risk Sharing, and the Importance of Imperfect Information', in Roumasset *et al.* (ed.) *Risk, Uncertainty and Agricultural Development*, Agricultural Development Council and South East Asian Regional Centre for Graduate Study and Research in Agriculture, Laguna, Philippines.

Omkarnath, G. (1993): *Rural Labour Processes: A Case Study in Coastal Andhra*, Doctoral Thesis, Centre for Economic Studies and Planning, Jawaharlal Nehru University, New Delhi.

Omkarnath, G. (2000): 'Wages in the Agrarian Economy', Unpublished Mimeo, Centre for Development Studies, Thiruvananthapuram.

Oommen, M.A (ed.) (1999): *Rethinking Development: Kerala's Development Experience,* Vol. I and II, Concept Publishing Company, New Delhi.

Osmani, S.R. (1991): 'Wage Determination in Rural Labour Markets: The Theory of Implicit Cooperation', *Journal of Development Economics,* Vol. 34.

Otsuka and Hayami (1988): 'Theories of Share Tenancy: A Critical Survey', *Economic Development and Cultural Change,* Vol. 37, No. 1.

Papola, T.S (1970): *Principles of Wage Determination: An Empirical Study,* Somaiya Publications Private Limited, Bombay.

Parameswaran, M.P. (1998): 'Kerala Model: What Does it Signify?' *Bulletin of Concerned Asian Scholars,* Vol. 30, No. 4.

Parayil, Govindan (ed.) (2000): *Kerala: The Development Experience—Reflections on Sustainability and Replicability,* Zed Books, London and New York.

Pothen, Jacob; Toms Joseph and K.T. George (2000): 'Plantation Management' in P.J. George and C. Kuruvilla Jacob (ed.), *"Natural Rubber: Agro Management and Crop Processing",* Rubber Research Institute of India, Kottayam.

Quibria, M.G. and Rashid, Salim (1984): 'The Puzzle of Sharecropping: A Survey of Theories', *World Development,* Vol. 12, No. 12.

Ramachandran, V.K. (1996): 'On Kerala's Development Achievements', in Dreze, J. and Sen, A. (ed.), *Indian Development: Selected Regional Perspectives,* Oxford University Press, Delhi.

Rao, J.M (1988): 'Fragmented Rural Labour Markets', *Journal of Political Studies,* Vol. 15, No. 2.

Remesh, Babu P. (2000): 'Rural Wages: On Developing an Analytical Framework', *NLI Research Study Series,* No. 7, V.V. Giri National Labour Institute, NOIDA.

Remesh, Babu P. (2003): 'Changing Consciousness and Image of Kerala Labour in the 20th Century', *Labour and Development,* Vol. 9, No. 1

Richard, Alan and Martin, Philip L. (1983): 'Introduction' in Richards and Martin (ed.), *Migration, Mechanisation and Agricultural Labour Markets in Egypt,* The American University in Cairo Press, Egypt.

Rodgers, G.B. (1975): 'Nutritionally Based Wage Determination in the Low-Income Labour Market', *Oxford Economic Papers*, No. 27.

Roumasset, James A. and Uy, Marilou (1980): 'Piece Rates, Time Rates, and Teams: Explaining Patterns in Employment Relation', *Journal of Economic Behaviour and Organisation*, Vol. 1, No. 1.

Rubber Board (1998): 'Labour Welfare Schemes of the Rubber Board, 1988-89', Rubber Board, Kottayam.

Rubber Board (2000): 'Rubber Grower's Companion 2000', Rubber Board, Kottayam.

Rubber Board (2003): *'Indian Rubber Statistics'*, Vol. 24, Rubber Board, Kottayam.

Rudra, Ashok (1982): 'Extra Economic Constraint on Agricultural Labour: Results of an Intensive Survey in Some Villages near Santiniketan, West Bengal', *Asian Employment Programme Working Paper*, ARTEP, ILO, New Delhi.

Saith, A. (1992): 'The Rural Non-Farm Economy, Processes and Policies', ILO, World Employment Programme, Geneva.

Scoones, I. (1998): 'Sustainable Rural Livelihoods: A Framework for Analysis' *IDS Working Paper*, No. 72, Institute of Development Studies, Brighton.

Scott, James C. (1976): *The Moral Economy of the Peasant*, Yale University Press, New Haven.

Shavell, Steven (1979): 'Risk Sharing and Incentives in the Principal and Agent Relationship', *Bell Journal of Economics*, Vol. 10, No. 1.

Singh, Nirvikar (1989): 'Theories of Sharecropping", in Bardhan, P.K. (ed.), *The Economic Theory of Agrarian Institutions*, Clarendon Press, Oxford.

Solow, R.M. (1990): 'The Labour Market as a Social Institution', Oxford, Black Well.

Stiglitz, J.E. (1974): 'Alternative Theories of Wage Determination and Unemployment in LDCs The Labour Turnover Model', *Quarterly Journal of Economics*, Vol. 88.

Stiglitz, J.E. (1976): 'The Efficiency Wage Hypothesis, Surplus Labour, and the Distribution of Income in LDCs', *Oxford Economic Papers*, No. 28.

Stirati, A. (1994): *Theory of Wages in Classical Economics,* Edward Elgar, Cheltenham.

Subrahmanian, K.K. (1994): 'Some Facets of the Manufacturing Industry in Kerala'. in Prakash, B.A. (ed.), *Kerala's Economy: Performance, Problems, Prospects,* Sage, New Delhi.

Tharamangalam, Joseph. (1998): 'The Perils of Social Development without Economic Growth: The Development Debacle of Kerala, India'. *Bulletin of Concerned Asian Scholars,* Vol. 30, No. 1.

UN/CDS (1975): 'Poverty, Unemployment and Development Policy: A Case Study of Selected Issues with Reference to Kerala', Unpublished Study Report, Centre for Development Studies, Trivandrum.

Unni, J. (1988): 'Agricultural Labourers in Rural Labour Households, 1956-57 to 1977-78, Changes in Employment, Wages and Incomes', *Economic and Political Weekly,* Vol. 23, No. 26.

Usha Devi, T.V. and Jayachandran V.N. (2001): 'Socio Economic Profile of Rubber Tappers in the Small Holding Sector. A Study of Kanjirappally Panchayat', Mimeo, Kerala Research Programme on Local Level Development, CDS, Trivandrum.

Viswanathan, P.K., George, K. Tharian and Joseph, Toms (2003): 'Informal Labour Market and Structural Devolution', *Economic and Political Weekly,* Vol. 38, No. 31

Waite, Louise (2001), 'Kerala's Informal Labour Market Interventions: From Work to Well-Being?', *Economic and Political Weekly,* Vol. 36, No. 26.

Yellen, J. L. (1984): 'Efficiency Wage Models of Unemployment', *American Economic Review,* Vol. 74.

Zachariah K.C.; Prakash, B.A and Rajan, S.I (2002): 'Gulf Migration Study: Employment, Wages and Working Conditions of Kerala Emigrants in the United Arab Emirates', *Working Paper,* No. 326, Centre for Development Studies, Trivandrum.

Index